Bigfoot: The Comprehensive Investigation into the Elusive Legend

Oliver Lancaster

Published by Oliver Lancaster, 2023.

BIGFOOT: THE COMPREHENSIVE INVESTIGATION INTO THE ELUSIVE LEGEND

First edition. July 9, 2023.

ISBN: 979-8215018217

Written by Oliver Lancaster.

Also by Oliver Lancaster

Chernobyl: Unveiling the tragedy. A Comprehensive Account of the Nuclear Disaster

The Bhopal Gas Tragedy: Unraveling the Catastrophe of 1984

The Deepwater Horizon Oil Spill of 2010: A Disaster Unveiled

Fukushima Fallout: Unveiling the Truth behind the 2011 Nuclear Disaster

Minamata Disease: Poisoned Waters and the Battle for Justice (1932-1968)

Evil Women: Unmasking History's Most Notorious Women

Bundy The Dark Chronicles: America's Infamous Serial Killer

Dahmer The Dark Chronicles: America's Infamous Milwaukee Cannibal

Zodiac The Dark Chronicles: America's Infamous Cryptic Killer

Bigfoot: The Comprehensive Investigation into the Elusive Legend

Watch for more at https://tinyurl.com/olanc.

Sign up to my free newsletter to get updates on new releases, FREE teaser chapters to upcoming releases and FREE digital short stories.

Or visit https://tinyurl.com/olanc

I never spam and you can unsubscribe at any time.

OLIVER LANCASTER

Disclaimer

The information presented in this book is based on extensive research and available evidence. While efforts have been made to present a comprehensive and balanced view of the Bigfoot phenomenon, readers are encouraged to approach the subject with an open mind. The views and opinions expressed by individuals and experts interviewed in this book are their own and do not necessarily reflect the views of the author or publisher. The existence of Bigfoot or any other cryptid mentioned in this book cannot be conclusively proven or disproven.

Bigfoot: The Comprehensive Investigation into the Elusive Legend

OLIVER LANCASTER

Chapter 1: Bigfoot through the Ages

Since time immemorial, stories of a mysterious creature lurking in the dense forests and rugged mountains have captivated the human imagination. Known by various names across different cultures, one particular enigma stands tall among them all: Bigfoot. With an aura of intrigue and an air of elusiveness, Bigfoot has become an enduring legend that continues to captivate believers and skeptics alike. In this section, we embark on a journey through time, unraveling the historical and cultural references that shed light on the origins and evolution of this elusive creature.

Ancient Legends:

The allure of Bigfoot can be traced back to ancient times, where indigenous cultures around the world shared tales of large, hairy beings residing in the wilderness. In Native American folklore, tribes such as the Chehalis, Salish, and Lummi spoke of Sasquatch, a towering creature dwelling in the Pacific Northwest. These legends described Sasquatch as a creature possessing great strength, stealth, and a deep spiritual connection to nature. Similar legends can be found in other parts of the world, such as the Yeti in the Himalayas and the Yowie in Australia.

European Encounters:

As European explorers set foot on new lands, encounters with Bigfoot-like creatures emerged in their accounts. The famous explorer, Marco Polo, documented encounters with hairy wild men during his travels in the 13th century. Likewise, during the Age of Exploration, European explorers reported encounters with "wild men" in the uncharted territories of North America. These encounters fueled speculation about the existence of an unknown species, bridging the gap between ancient legends and modern-day Bigfoot sightings.

Scientific Inquiry and Expedition:

The 19th and 20th centuries witnessed a shift in the perception of Bigfoot from folklore to a subject of scientific inquiry. In 1847, a publication called "The Wild Man" circulated in newspapers, discussing a creature seen in the forests of North America. This marked one of the first instances where a public conversation about Bigfoot occurred in the context of science. Fast forward to the mid-20th century, and interest in Bigfoot surged again with the highly publicized 1958 discovery of large footprints in Bluff Creek, California.

Prominent Figures and Investigations:

Throughout the years, numerous individuals have dedicated their lives to investigating Bigfoot and gathering evidence of its existence. One of the most notable figures in the Bigfoot research community is Dr. Grover Krantz, a physical anthropologist who believed that Bigfoot could be a surviving species of Gigantopithecus, an extinct giant ape. Dr. Krantz's research and expertise brought a scientific rigor to the study of Bigfoot.

In the 1960s, a couple named Roger and Bob captured a now-iconic film known as the Patterson-Gimlin film, which purportedly shows a female Bigfoot walking through the woods. Despite skepticism and debate surrounding its authenticity, the film remains one of the most influential pieces of evidence in the Bigfoot lore.

Modern Pop Culture and Media:

Bigfoot's presence in popular culture grew exponentially in the latter half of the 20th century and continues to thrive in the digital age. From movies and documentaries to reality TV shows, Bigfoot has become a staple in the entertainment industry. Notable examples include the TV series "Finding Bigfoot" and the film franchise "Harry and the Hendersons." These portrayals, although often fictionalized, have played a significant role in perpetuating the legend and fueling public fascination with Bigfoot.

As we delve into the historical and cultural references surrounding Bigfoot, it becomes evident that the legend of this elusive creature is deeply ingrained in human consciousness. Ancient legends, European encounters, scientific inquiry, and popular media have all contributed to shaping the multifaceted nature of the Bigfoot phenomenon. In the following sections, we will further explore the evidence, theories, and ongoing investigations that seek to unravel the mystery behind Bigfoot, providing a comprehensive investigation into this enigmatic legend.

Throughout history, various cultures around the world have shared legends and folklore about elusive creatures similar to Bigfoot. These ancient tales provide valuable insights into the universal fascination with mysterious, hairy beings that inhabit the remote corners of our planet. In this section, we delve into the rich tapestry of ancient legends and folklore surrounding similar creatures, shedding light on the enduring human fascination with these enigmatic beings.

The Yeti of the Himalayas:

Nestled high in the snowy peaks of the Himalayas, the legendary Yeti, also known as the Abominable Snowman, has captivated the imaginations of locals and adventurers alike. According to Himalayan folklore, the Yeti is a towering creature covered in shaggy hair, possessing immense strength and agility. Tales of the Yeti often describe encounters with footprints, hair samples, and eerie vocalizations echoing through the mountains. Sherpas and Tibetan Buddhists regard the Yeti as a sacred creature, embodying both fear and reverence.

The Yowie of Australia:

In the vast and untamed wilderness of Australia, ancient Aboriginal legends speak of the Yowie, a creature bearing striking similarities to Bigfoot. Aboriginal folklore describes the Yowie as a large, hairy humanoid inhabiting the dense forests and rugged mountain ranges. Stories recount encounters with this elusive being, characterized by its imposing stature, long arms, and distinctive footprints. The Yowie is often depicted as a guardian of the land, a mysterious creature embodying both fear and respect in Aboriginal culture.

The Almas of Central Asia:

Traversing the desolate landscapes of Central Asia, legends of the Almas have intrigued nomadic tribes for centuries. Known by various names across different regions, the Almas is believed to be a wild, hairy humanoid that dwells in the remote mountain ranges. Stories depict the Almas as a reclusive creature, displaying remarkable strength and agility. Nomadic tribes recount encounters with the Almas, describing its imposing size, piercing eyes, and uncanny ability to vanish without a trace. These tales continue to be passed down through generations, preserving the mystique surrounding this ancient legend.

The Skunk Ape of North America:

In the swamps and dense forests of North America, the legend of the Skunk Ape emerges from the depths of folklore. Similar to Bigfoot, the Skunk Ape is described as a large, ape-like creature covered in dark hair, exuding a pungent odor that lends it its name. Sightings of the Skunk Ape have been reported primarily in the southern United States, particularly in Florida. Witnesses describe its massive size, distinct odor, and ability to move silently through the dense vegetation. The Skunk Ape's legend intertwines with Native American folklore, as various tribes recount encounters with similar hairy beings in the wilderness.

The Mapinguari of South America:

Deep within the dense rainforests of South America, the Mapinguari roams the imaginations of indigenous tribes. Described as a massive creature standing upright on two legs, the Mapinguari possesses long claws and thick, matted fur that serves as armor against predators. Legends of the Mapinguari often warn against venturing too deep into the forest, as encounters with this fearsome creature are said to bring calamity upon those who disturb its domain. These tales, steeped in mysticism and reverence for the natural world, remind us of the enduring connection between ancient cultures and the mythical creatures that inhabit their lands.

Ancient legends and folklore from around the world paint a vivid picture of creatures similar to Bigfoot, captivating the human imagination across time and space. The tales of the Yeti, Yowie, Almas, Skunk Ape, and Mapinguari reveal a shared fascination with enigmatic, hairy beings that dwell in the remote corners of our planet. These legends not only provide cultural richness but also serve as a testament to the profound and enduring connection humans have with the mysteries of the natural world. In the next section, we will delve into scientific investigations and evidence that have sought to shed light on the existence of these elusive creatures.

BIGFOOT: THE COMPREHENSIVE INVESTIGATION INTO THE ELUSIVE LEGEND

13

Chapter 2: Defining Bigfoot

The enigmatic legend of Bigfoot has been shaped by numerous eyewitness accounts, alleged sightings, and collected evidence over the years. This section aims to explore the commonly reported characteristics and physical features associated with Bigfoot, providing an overview of the creature's purported appearance and abilities. While the details may vary across different accounts, a set of distinct traits has emerged, contributing to the enduring image of this elusive creature.

Physical Description:

Bigfoot, also known as Sasquatch, is generally described as a large, bipedal humanoid covered in thick, matted hair or fur. The creature's height is commonly reported to range from 7 to 10 feet (2 to 3 meters), making it significantly taller than an average human. Witnesses often describe Bigfoot as possessing a robust, muscular build, suggesting immense strength and physical prowess. The hair color is frequently described as dark brown or black, though variations in coloration have been reported.

Head and Facial Features:

Bigfoot is often described as having a large, ape-like head, proportionate to its massive body. Witnesses frequently note a prominent, sloping forehead and a pronounced brow ridge, similar to that of an early hominid. The face of Bigfoot is commonly described as having a flat, broad nose and a wide mouth, which some witnesses claim has visible lips. Reports vary regarding the presence of hair or fur on the face, with some witnesses stating that the creature has hair covering the entire face, while others suggest bare or sparsely haired features.

Eyes:

The eyes of Bigfoot are often a subject of fascination and speculation. Witnesses describe them as large and expressive, conveying a sense of intelligence and curiosity. The color of the eyes is commonly reported to be dark, ranging from brown to black. The reflective quality of the eyes at night has been noted in numerous accounts, adding to the mystery and eerie allure of the creature.

Limbs and Hands:

Bigfoot's limbs are reported to be well-muscled and proportionate to its massive frame. Witnesses frequently describe long, powerful arms that hang down past the creature's knees. The hands of Bigfoot are often mentioned as having opposable thumbs, enabling it to grasp and manipulate objects. The fingers are reported to be thick and sturdy, possibly aiding in tree climbing or other activities.

Footprints:

One of the most compelling pieces of evidence associated with Bigfoot are the footprints attributed to the creature. These footprints are characterized by their size and distinctive features. They often measure between 15 to 24 inches (38 to

61 centimeters) in length and exhibit a pronounced arch. Witnesses note that the footprints show a resemblance to a human foot, but with significantly greater size and breadth. The number of toes is commonly reported as five, and the footprints often exhibit dermal ridges and toe impressions.

Other Physical Traits:

Additional physical features have been reported in conjunction with Bigfoot sightings. Witnesses mention a strong, musky odor emanating from the creature, sometimes likened to a combination of wet fur, decaying matter, and a pungent stench. This odor has been associated with encounters in various regions and is considered by some to be a distinct characteristic of Bigfoot.

The physical characteristics commonly associated with Bigfoot depict a massive, bipedal creature covered in thick, matted hair. Witnesses describe its towering height, muscular build, and distinctive facial features. The creature's eyes, limbs, and hands are often noted for their size, strength, and potential similarities to both humans and apes. The footprints attributed to Bigfoot have provided intriguing evidence, showcasing large impressions with dermal ridges and toe imprints. While the details may vary across different accounts, these shared characteristics contribute to the collective image of Bigfoot, an elusive creature that continues to capture the imagination and curiosity of people around the world. In the subsequent sections, we will explore the evidence and theories surrounding the existence of Bigfoot, delving deeper into the ongoing investigation of this enduring legend.

Eyewitness accounts play a crucial role in shaping our understanding of Bigfoot, providing firsthand testimonies of encounters with the elusive creature. While individual accounts may vary in their details, patterns and similarities emerge when analyzing a collection of reports. In this section, we will delve into various eyewitness accounts of Bigfoot sightings and explore the commonalities that arise, offering insights into the shared experiences and characteristics associated with these encounters.

Size and Height:

A recurring theme in eyewitness accounts is the sheer size and height of Bigfoot. Witnesses consistently describe encountering a creature that surpasses the height of an average human, often ranging from 7 to 10 feet (2 to 3 meters) tall. This consistency across reports suggests a consistent pattern in the perceived stature of Bigfoot, emphasizing its imposing presence.

Physical Appearance:

Eyewitnesses commonly describe Bigfoot as a large, bipedal creature covered in hair or fur. The coloration of the hair is often reported as dark brown or black, aligning with the popular image of a hulking, hairy creature. Witnesses note the thickness and unkempt nature of the hair, with some accounts mentioning matted or shaggy fur. These consistent descriptions of Bigfoot's physical appearance contribute to the formation of a recognizable and shared image of the creature.

Facial Features:

BIGFOOT: THE COMPREHENSIVE INVESTIGATION INTO THE ELUSIVE LEGEND

While there may be variation in the specifics, several recurring facial features emerge from eyewitness accounts. Witnesses frequently mention a prominent forehead and brow ridge, giving the impression of an elongated or sloping forehead. The eyes of Bigfoot are often described as large and expressive, conveying a sense of intelligence or curiosity. Reports of a wide, flat nose and a wide mouth with visible lips also surface, contributing to the composite image of Bigfoot's facial characteristics.

Limbs and Gait:

Eyewitnesses commonly note the proportions and movements of Bigfoot's limbs. The creature is often described as having long, muscular arms that hang down past its knees. Witnesses frequently emphasize the creature's powerful strides and the smooth, fluid motion of its gait. The limbs are reported to exhibit strength and agility, contributing to the perception of Bigfoot as a formidable and physically adept creature.

Behavior and Vocalizations:

Witnesses often recount specific behaviors and vocalizations associated with Bigfoot encounters. Many describe the creature as exhibiting a cautious and elusive nature, often vanishing quickly into the wilderness after being spotted. Reports of tree shaking, wood knocking, and vocalizations such as growls, howls, or deep guttural sounds are common. These behaviors and vocalizations contribute to the perception of Bigfoot as a wild, primal entity, deeply ingrained in its natural environment.

Footprints and Physical Evidence:

One of the most compelling aspects of eyewitness accounts is the discovery of footprints and other physical evidence left behind by Bigfoot. Witnesses often describe encountering large footprints, exhibiting characteristics such as a pronounced arch, dermal ridges, and toe impressions. The consistency in the size, shape, and distinctive features of these footprints across various accounts strengthens the credibility of the evidence. In some instances, witnesses report finding hair samples, nests, or other potential signs of Bigfoot's presence, further supporting their claims.

Analyzing a collection of eyewitness accounts reveals commonalities and shared experiences surrounding encounters with Bigfoot. Witnesses consistently describe a towering creature, surpassing human height, with a large, hairy body and distinctive facial features. Reports highlight the creature's powerful limbs, fluid gait, and elusive behavior. The presence of footprints and other physical evidence adds weight to these testimonies. While individual details may vary, the recurring patterns provide a basis for understanding the shared characteristics associated with Bigfoot encounters. In the next sections, we will explore the scientific investigations, evidence, and theories that have been put forth to shed light on the existence and nature of this elusive creature.

Chapter 3: Cryptozoology and Bigfoot

In the pursuit of uncovering hidden creatures that defy scientific classification, the field of cryptozoology has emerged as a bridge between folklore, eyewitness accounts, and scientific inquiry. Cryptozoology, which literally means "the study of hidden animals," seeks to investigate and document creatures that have not been recognized or fully understood by mainstream science. Bigfoot, with its rich history of sightings and legends, stands as one of the prime subjects within the realm of cryptozoology. In this section, we will explore the field of cryptozoology and its relationship to the investigation of Bigfoot.

Cryptozoology is an interdisciplinary field that blends elements of biology, zoology, anthropology, and folklore to investigate and validate the existence of cryptids, which are creatures that have yet to be recognized by science. These cryptids include legendary creatures like Bigfoot, the Loch Ness Monster, the Chupacabra, and many others. Cryptozoologists approach their work by examining eyewitness accounts, analyzing purported evidence, conducting field research, and exploring the cultural and historical contexts surrounding these creatures.

Within the realm of cryptozoology, the investigation of Bigfoot occupies a prominent position. Bigfoot, with its long history of sightings and cultural significance, has become one of the most well-known and enduring cryptids. Cryptozoologists interested in Bigfoot study the vast body of eyewitness accounts, track reported sightings, analyze footprint casts, and explore areas with a high frequency of alleged encounters. They strive to collect evidence and build a comprehensive understanding of the creature's behavior, habitat, and potential existence.

Cryptozoology faces inherent challenges in its pursuit of creatures like Bigfoot. The elusive nature of cryptids makes their study difficult, as they are often encountered unexpectedly or fleetingly. Additionally, the scarcity of tangible physical evidence, such as DNA or carcasses, presents obstacles to traditional scientific validation. Critics argue that the lack of conclusive evidence undermines the legitimacy of cryptozoology as a scientific field. However, proponents of cryptozoology emphasize the importance of open-mindedness, cultural exploration, and the potential for discovering new species or understanding undiscovered aspects of known species.

Cryptozoology exists at the fringes of mainstream science due to its exploration of unverified or unaccepted creatures. Skeptics within the scientific community argue that the focus on cryptids, including Bigfoot, diverts attention and resources from more well-established areas of scientific study. They contend that the lack of robust evidence and reproducibility impedes the scientific rigor that characterizes mainstream research. However, some scientists acknowledge the value of cryptozoology in engaging the public's curiosity, preserving cultural heritage, and potentially uncovering new species or ecological insights.

Over time, cryptozoology has evolved to incorporate new methodologies and technologies in its investigations. DNA analysis, footprint analysis, thermal imaging, and audio recording devices have allowed researchers to collect and analyze potential evidence with greater precision. Advances in communication and collaboration have also enabled cryptozoologists to connect and share data globally, enhancing their efforts to study and document cryptids like Bigfoot.

Cryptozoology provides a platform for the investigation of creatures that exist in the realm of folklore and eyewitness accounts, with Bigfoot serving as a prominent subject of study. While facing skepticism from mainstream science, cryptozoologists are driven by a passion to explore the mysteries of the natural world and uncover potential hidden species. The field offers an interdisciplinary approach, combining scientific methodologies with cultural and historical perspectives. As technology advances and exploration continues, cryptozoology may yet provide insights into the existence and nature of enigmatic creatures like Bigfoot. In the following sections, we will explore the evidence and theories that have been put forth in the quest to unravel the mystery of Bigfoot.

The world of cryptozoology is replete with tales of elusive creatures that capture the imagination and fuel the curiosity of enthusiasts. While Bigfoot stands as one of the most renowned cryptids, numerous other creatures share similar characteristics and cultural significance. In this section, we will explore some of the most famous cryptids from around the world, highlighting their parallels to Bigfoot and the shared fascination they evoke.

1. Yeti or Abominable Snowman:

The Yeti, also known as the Abominable Snowman, inhabits the treacherous peaks of the Himalayas. Much like Bigfoot, the Yeti is described as a towering, bipedal creature covered in shaggy hair. Witnesses report sightings, footprints, and tales passed down through generations, portraying the Yeti as an elusive and formidable being. Both the Yeti and Bigfoot share similar physical attributes and evoke a sense of mystery and wonder.

2. Loch Ness Monster:

The Loch Ness Monster, often referred to as "Nessie," is a legendary creature said to inhabit Loch Ness in Scotland. Although different in appearance from Bigfoot, Nessie captures the public's imagination much like its terrestrial counterpart. Similar to Bigfoot sightings, numerous eyewitness accounts and controversial photographs claim to depict the creature. Both Nessie and Bigfoot represent enduring mysteries and continue to inspire exploration and speculation.

3. Chupacabra:

The Chupacabra, a cryptid prevalent in Latin American folklore, is known for its alleged attacks on livestock. Though physically distinct from Bigfoot, the Chupacabra is often described as a creature with spines or quills along its back, large eyes, and a reptilian appearance. Like Bigfoot, the Chupacabra has been the subject of numerous eyewitness accounts and investigations, contributing to its enduring status as a cryptid of intrigue.

4. Mothman:

The Mothman is a creature associated with sightings in Point Pleasant, West Virginia, during the 1960s. While visually distinct from Bigfoot, the Mothman shares parallels in terms of its elusive nature and impact on local folklore. Witnesses describe the Mothman as a tall, winged creature with glowing red eyes. Sightings of the Mothman were often accompanied by reports of strange phenomena, adding to its mystique and connection to the realm of the unknown.

5. Jersey Devil:

The Jersey Devil is a cryptid from the Pine Barrens of New Jersey, United States. This legendary creature is described as having a horse-like body, bat-like wings, hooves, and a head resembling that of a goat. Despite its physical differences, the Jersey Devil is akin to Bigfoot in terms of its cultural significance and the plethora of reported sightings. The legend of the Jersey Devil has become deeply ingrained in New Jersey folklore, captivating generations of locals and enthusiasts alike.

While Bigfoot stands as a preeminent figure within the realm of cryptozoology, other famous cryptids share striking parallels and cultural significance. The Yeti, Loch Ness Monster, Chupacabra, Mothman, and Jersey Devil each possess their own unique characteristics and legends, yet evoke a similar sense of intrigue and mystery. These cryptids, like Bigfoot, inspire curiosity, exploration, and debates within the realm of cryptozoology. As enthusiasts and researchers delve into the world of hidden creatures, the pursuit of these cryptids continues to captivate imaginations and fuel the desire to uncover the truth behind these enduring legends.

Chapter 4: Bigfoot Sightings: An Overview

Bigfoot, the elusive creature of legend and lore, has sparked fascination and curiosity across the globe. In this section, we will explore some of the most famous Bigfoot sightings throughout history. These sightings have left an indelible mark on the Bigfoot phenomenon, contributing to the ongoing investigation and speculation surrounding this enigmatic creature.

1. Ape Canyon Incident (1924):

One of the earliest notable Bigfoot sightings occurred in 1924, when a group of miners known as the Ape Canyon miners claimed to have encountered a group of large, hairy, man-like creatures in the remote area of Ape Canyon, Washington. According to their accounts, the creatures pelted their cabin with rocks, leading to a harrowing night filled with fear and desperation. The incident generated widespread interest, capturing the public's imagination and fueling speculation about the existence of Bigfoot.

2. The Patterson-Gimlin Film (1967):

Arguably the most iconic piece of evidence in the Bigfoot lore is the Patterson-Gimlin film, captured on October 20, 1967, in Bluff Creek, California. Roger Patterson and Bob Gimlin filmed a purported female Bigfoot, commonly referred to as

"Patty," walking through a clearing. The film shows a creature with a distinctive gait, towering height, and covered in hair. Despite ongoing debates regarding its authenticity, the Patterson-Gimlin film remains a pivotal moment in Bigfoot research, shaping popular perception and inspiring countless investigations.

3. Skookum Cast (2000):

In 2000, a significant discovery known as the Skookum Cast brought attention to Bigfoot research. The cast was made from an impression found in the mud near the Skookum Meadows area of Washington State. Measuring approximately four feet in length, the cast appeared to show the imprint of a large, primate-like foot. The Skookum Cast sparked debates among experts, with some arguing that it could provide evidence of Bigfoot's existence. While skeptics proposed alternative explanations, the cast remains a subject of interest and discussion in the Bigfoot research community.

4. Freeman Footage (1994):

In 1994, a video footage known as the Freeman Footage emerged, capturing a potential Bigfoot sighting in the forests of Ohio. The footage, shot by Paul Freeman, depicts a large, hairy creature walking among the trees. Though the quality of the video is not pristine, it garnered attention within the Bigfoot community and fueled ongoing debates about its authenticity. The Freeman Footage remains one of the more widely known and analyzed pieces of visual evidence in Bigfoot research.

5. Sierra Sounds (1971):

BIGFOOT: THE COMPREHENSIVE INVESTIGATION INTO THE ELUSIVE LEGEND

The Sierra Sounds, recorded in the Sierra Nevada Mountains of California in 1971 by Ron Morehead and Alan Berry, captured a series of vocalizations believed to be made by Bigfoot. The recordings feature a range of haunting and unusual sounds, including whoops, growls, and vocalizations resembling a primate language. While skeptics question the origin and authenticity of the recordings, they have intrigued researchers and enthusiasts, contributing to the ongoing exploration of Bigfoot vocalizations.

These famous Bigfoot sightings throughout history have played a significant role in shaping the legend and perpetuating the investigation of this elusive creature. From the Ape Canyon Incident in 1924 to the Patterson-Gimlin film in 1967 and subsequent discoveries, each sighting has left an indelible mark on the Bigfoot phenomenon. Whether through visual evidence, audio recordings, or compelling firsthand accounts, these sightings have captivated the public's imagination, inspiring further research, and fueling the ongoing quest to unravel the mystery of Bigfoot. In the next sections, we will delve deeper into the evidence, theories, and ongoing investigations surrounding this enigmatic creature.

In the search for evidence of Bigfoot's existence, various forms of documentation have emerged, ranging from footprints to photographs and video footage. While skepticism and debate surround each piece of evidence, some have been regarded as credible and compelling within the realm of Bigfoot research. In this section, we will examine notable examples of footprints, photographs, and video footage that have contributed to the ongoing discourse surrounding Bigfoot.

Footprints are often considered one of the most tangible forms of evidence in Bigfoot research. Numerous footprint casts have been collected over the years, exhibiting characteristics consistent with descriptions of Bigfoot. These casts often showcase a large size, ranging from 15 to 24 inches (38 to 61 centimeters) in length, with distinct features such as a pronounced arch, dermal ridges, and toe impressions. Notable examples include the 1958 Bluff Creek footprints discovered by Jerry Crew, which sparked widespread interest and initiated a renewed focus on the study of Bigfoot. Subsequent footprint finds have added to the body of evidence, supporting claims of a large, bipedal creature roaming remote areas.

Photographs purporting to capture Bigfoot have been both celebrated and scrutinized. Among the most famous is the Patterson-Gimlin film from 1967, which documented a purported female Bigfoot known as "Patty." While debates persist regarding its authenticity, the film remains influential due to the creature's unique gait, size, and apparent coverage of hair. Other photographs, such as the Freeman Footage and various still images, have also garnered attention and analysis within the Bigfoot research community. Despite skeptics offering alternative explanations and potential hoaxes, these photographs have contributed to the visual record and public awareness of Bigfoot.

Video footage has played a significant role in shaping public perception and generating interest in Bigfoot. The aforementioned Patterson-Gimlin film is a hallmark example, capturing the creature's distinct movements and physical features. While skeptics question its legitimacy, the film has withstood decades of scrutiny and analysis. Additionally, video recordings like the Freeman Footage and various user-generated content continue to emerge, often showing fleeting glimpses of large, hairy figures in remote locations. While the quality and authenticity of such footage vary, they continue to fuel the ongoing investigation and debate surrounding Bigfoot.

The examination of credible evidence is not without its challenges and skeptics. Critics argue that footprints can be faked, photographs can be manipulated, and video footage can be staged. They highlight the lack of definitive scientific analysis or peer-reviewed studies confirming the existence of Bigfoot. Skeptics suggest that footprint casts can be produced using wooden carvings or other methods, and that photographs and video footage can be easily fabricated in an era of advanced technology. The absence of a verifiable specimen or conclusive DNA evidence further contributes to the skepticism surrounding Bigfoot.

While the examination of credible evidence such as footprints, photographs, and video footage forms a crucial aspect of Bigfoot research, it remains a subject of ongoing debate and skepticism. Footprints with distinct features, compelling photographs, and iconic video footage have emerged throughout history, shaping the discourse and capturing the public's imagination. However, critics argue that these forms of evidence can be susceptible to hoaxes or misinterpretation. The challenge lies in subjecting such evidence to rigorous scientific scrutiny and analysis, including independent verification, DNA testing, and comprehensive peer review. In the following sections, we will explore additional evidence, theories, and ongoing investigations that contribute to the quest for understanding the elusive creature known as Bigfoot.

Chapter 5: The Search for Bigfoot: Expeditions and Investigations

The quest to find concrete evidence of Bigfoot has led to numerous expeditions and research efforts undertaken by dedicated individuals and organizations. These endeavors aim to gather scientific data, conduct field investigations, and document potential encounters with the elusive creature. In this section, we will explore some of the notable expeditions and research initiatives that have contributed to the ongoing search for Bigfoot.

1. The Bigfoot Field Researchers Organization (BFRO):

The Bigfoot Field Researchers Organization, founded in 1995 by Matt Moneymaker, is one of the most prominent and active organizations dedicated to the study of Bigfoot. The BFRO organizes expeditions, conducts investigations, and collects reports from witnesses across North America. With a focus on scientific research, the organization encourages evidence-based documentation and employs field techniques such as footprint casting, audio recording, and visual surveillance. The BFRO's extensive database of reports and collaborative research efforts have contributed significantly to the body of knowledge surrounding Bigfoot.

2. The North American Wood Ape Conservancy (NAWAC):

The North American Wood Ape Conservancy is a group of researchers and enthusiasts dedicated to the study of Bigfoot, specifically focusing on an area known as the "Big Thicket" in Texas. The NAWAC employs scientific methods, including camera traps, audio recording devices, and field observation techniques, to gather data on the elusive creature. Their research efforts aim to better understand Bigfoot's behavior, habitat, and potential interactions with its environment. The NAWAC also collaborates with other organizations and shares findings within the scientific and cryptozoological communities.

3. The Olympic Project:

The Olympic Project, established in 2009, is a research group primarily focused on investigating Bigfoot sightings and activity within the Olympic Peninsula of Washington State. Comprising a team of researchers, biologists, and other experts, the Olympic Project employs a multidisciplinary approach to gather evidence and study the elusive creature. Their research methods include audio analysis, footprint analysis, and wildlife camera placement. The project aims to bridge the gap between mainstream scientific research and the study of Bigfoot by conducting systematic and rigorous investigations.

4. The Sasquatch Genome Project:

The Sasquatch Genome Project, led by Dr. Melba Ketchum, sought to provide genetic evidence of Bigfoot's existence. The project involved the collection and analysis of purported Bigfoot DNA samples, including hair, tissue, and other biological material. While the project generated controversy and criticism within the scientific community, it aimed to provide empirical evidence through DNA analysis. The findings and conclusions of the project remain a subject of ongoing debate and scrutiny.

5. Independent Research Expeditions:

Numerous independent researchers and enthusiasts have undertaken their own expeditions in search of Bigfoot. These expeditions often involve field investigations, exploration of reported hotspots, and engagement with local witnesses. Independent researchers employ a range of techniques, including audio recording, night vision surveillance, and the use of motion-triggered cameras. While these efforts may lack the resources and recognition of larger organizations, they contribute to the collective knowledge and provide a grassroots perspective on Bigfoot research.

Notable expeditions and research efforts dedicated to finding Bigfoot have brought together passionate individuals, organizations, and communities seeking to uncover the truth behind this elusive creature. The Bigfoot Field Researchers Organization, the North American Wood Ape Conservancy, the Olympic Project, the Sasquatch Genome Project, and independent researchers have employed a variety of scientific and investigative techniques to document evidence, gather data, and explore reported sightings and encounters. While the search for definitive proof of Bigfoot's existence continues, these expeditions and research initiatives contribute to the ongoing investigation and understanding of the enigmatic creature known as Bigfoot.

Bigfoot investigations require a diverse range of methods and technology to gather evidence, conduct field research, and document potential encounters. Researchers and enthusiasts employ a combination of traditional field techniques and advanced technology to aid in their quest to understand the elusive creature. In this section, we will explore some of the methods and technology commonly used in Bigfoot investigations.

Field observation and documentation form the backbone of Bigfoot investigations. Researchers spend time in areas with reported Bigfoot sightings, observing the environment, collecting data, and documenting their findings. This involves meticulous note-taking, sketching, and mapping of the area. Researchers strive to record details such as physical features, behavior, vocalizations, and any other relevant information. Field observations provide valuable firsthand accounts and contribute to the overall understanding of Bigfoot behavior and habitat.

Footprint analysis is a crucial component of Bigfoot investigations. Researchers meticulously examine footprints left behind by the creature, documenting their size, shape, and distinctive features. They use tools such as measuring tapes, calipers, and plaster casts to create accurate reproductions of the footprints. Analysis includes assessing dermal ridges, toe impressions, arch structure, and any other unique characteristics. This information helps determine the size, gait, and potential biological aspects of Bigfoot.

Audio recording plays a significant role in Bigfoot investigations. Researchers use high-quality audio recording devices to capture potential vocalizations, howls, growls, or other sounds associated with Bigfoot. Specialized microphones and audio equipment are employed to ensure clarity and minimize background noise. Recorded audio is later analyzed using software tools to identify patterns, frequency ranges, and potential similarities to known animal sounds or human vocalizations. This analysis aids in understanding Bigfoot communication and behavior.

Visual documentation, such as photography and videography, is a crucial aspect of Bigfoot investigations. Researchers use cameras, including digital cameras, video cameras, and thermal imaging devices, to capture potential visual evidence of Bigfoot. This includes capturing images or video footage of the creature, footprints, habitat, or any other relevant details. Advanced imaging technologies, such as high-resolution cameras and infrared cameras, help improve the quality and accuracy of visual documentation.

Camera traps are a commonly used tool in Bigfoot investigations. These motion-activated cameras are strategically placed in areas with reported Bigfoot activity or near potential feeding grounds, water sources, or travel routes. Camera traps can capture images or video footage when triggered by movement, providing a passive means of observation. These devices are often equipped with night vision capabilities, allowing for surveillance during low-light conditions. Camera traps offer researchers the opportunity to gather visual evidence without directly impacting the environment or alerting the creature to human presence.

Advancements in drone technology have made them a valuable tool in Bigfoot investigations. Drones equipped with high-resolution cameras and thermal imaging capabilities can survey large areas of difficult terrain, providing aerial footage and detailed imagery. Drones allow researchers to explore remote locations, inaccessible areas, or dense forested regions that might be challenging to access on foot. This technology expands the reach and efficiency of Bigfoot investigations, aiding in the documentation and exploration of potential sighting locations.

Bigfoot investigations utilize a combination of traditional field techniques and advanced technology to gather evidence and document potential encounters. Field observation and documentation, footprint analysis, audio recording and analysis, visual documentation, camera traps, and drone technology all play crucial roles in the pursuit of understanding Bigfoot. These methods and technology help researchers document physical evidence, capture visual and auditory data, and explore remote or challenging environments. By employing a multidisciplinary approach and leveraging technological advancements, investigators aim to shed light on the enigmatic creature known as Bigfoot.

Chapter 6: Bigfoot in the Scientific Community

The scientific community's perception of Bigfoot is characterized by skepticism and a cautious approach rooted in the scientific method. While the phenomenon captures public interest and intrigue, the scientific community often maintains a critical stance due to the lack of conclusive evidence and the presence of potential hoaxes. In this section, we will explore the scientific community's perception of Bigfoot, the challenges it poses, and the factors contributing to its skeptical stance.

One of the primary reasons for the scientific community's skepticism towards Bigfoot is the absence of definitive evidence supporting its existence. While there have been numerous eyewitness accounts, footprint casts, photographs, and video footage, these forms of evidence fall short of meeting the scientific standard for conclusive proof. The lack of physical remains, DNA samples, or unequivocal visual documentation hinders the scientific community's ability to conduct rigorous analysis and draw definitive conclusions.

Scientists approach the study of cryptids like Bigfoot with a focus on methodological rigor. The scientific method requires systematic data collection, analysis, and peer review to establish the validity of claims. The anecdotal nature of most Bigfoot sightings and the limitations of available evidence make it challenging to apply these scientific principles. Skeptics argue that the quality and reliability of eyewitness testimonies can be compromised by biases, misperceptions, or hoaxes. Without scientifically sound methodologies and verifiable evidence, the scientific community remains cautious in embracing the existence of Bigfoot.

The association of Bigfoot with folklore, legends, and cultural narratives also contributes to the scientific community's skepticism. Cryptids often occupy a realm of cultural mythology and popular imagination, which can blur the lines between scientific inquiry and folklore. The scientific community generally approaches phenomena from an empirical standpoint, demanding evidence that can be tested, observed, and reproduced. The intertwining of Bigfoot with storytelling and cultural beliefs creates a complex backdrop that scientists find challenging to navigate when assessing the creature's existence.

The scientific community's focus and allocation of resources are often directed towards well-established fields of study and research areas. Bigfoot investigations, perceived by some as fringe or lacking in scientific credibility, may struggle to secure significant funding or attract mainstream scientific interest. The limited resources available for dedicated research and comprehensive investigations pose challenges for scientists who wish to study Bigfoot within the accepted frameworks of scientific inquiry.

Scientists are mindful of their professional reputation and the credibility of their work. The study of Bigfoot and other cryptids can be viewed as controversial or outside the mainstream scientific discourse. Engaging in research on subjects that lack broad scientific acceptance may carry risks in terms of professional reputation or the potential for being marginalized within the scientific community. Consequently, many scientists may be hesitant to associate themselves with research endeavors focused on Bigfoot.

The scientific community's perception of Bigfoot is generally skeptical due to the lack of conclusive evidence, methodological concerns, cultural influences, limited funding, and concerns about reputation and credibility. While there may be individual scientists who maintain an open-minded interest in the subject, the broader scientific community awaits substantial and verifiable evidence before considering Bigfoot as a legitimate field of study. As investigations continue and potential evidence emerges, it will be critical to adhere to rigorous scientific standards, engage in collaborative research efforts, and employ objective methodologies to bridge the gap between scientific skepticism and the quest for understanding the mysteries surrounding Bigfoot.

While skepticism prevails in the scientific community regarding Bigfoot, there have been notable scientists and researchers who have dedicated their efforts to studying the phenomenon. These individuals have approached Bigfoot investigations with scientific rigor, employing diverse methodologies and contributing to the body of knowledge surrounding this elusive creature. In this section, we will explore some of the notable scientists and researchers who have engaged in Bigfoot studies.

1. Dr. Grover Krantz (1931-2002):

Dr. Grover Krantz was a respected physical anthropologist and professor at Washington State University. He became intrigued by Bigfoot after examining footprint casts and conducting his own investigations. Krantz believed that Bigfoot could represent an undiscovered species of hominid and dedicated considerable time and resources to researching the subject. He analyzed footprint casts, advocated for the collection of more physical evidence, and proposed theories on Bigfoot's biology and behavior. While his views were met with skepticism, Krantz remains a prominent figure in Bigfoot research due to his scientific background and dedication to the field.

2. Dr. Jeff Meldrum:

Dr. Jeff Meldrum is a professor of anatomy and anthropology at Idaho State University and one of the most recognizable scientists associated with Bigfoot studies. He has extensively researched the biomechanics and morphology of bipedalism, focusing on the analysis of footprints attributed to Bigfoot. Meldrum has examined numerous footprint casts, conducting detailed investigations into their characteristics, dermal ridges, and potential indicators of a genuine biological origin. He has also authored books on the subject and advocates for further scientific investigation into the existence of Bigfoot.

3. Dr. John Bindernagel (1941-2018):

Dr. John Bindernagel was a wildlife biologist who devoted much of his career to studying the existence of Bigfoot. His background in wildlife research provided a scientific foundation for his interest in the creature. Bindernagel conducted field investigations, interviewed witnesses, and examined footprint casts. He believed that Bigfoot could represent an unrecognized primate species and called for increased scientific attention to the phenomenon. Bindernagel's research and writings have contributed to the scientific discourse surrounding Bigfoot.

4. Dr. Esteban Sarmiento:

Dr. Esteban Sarmiento is a biological anthropologist and primatologist who has lent his expertise to Bigfoot studies. He has examined footprint casts, assessed the potential biological characteristics of Bigfoot, and offered insights based on his knowledge of primate anatomy and behavior. Sarmiento has highlighted the importance of conducting systematic and rigorous investigations into the phenomenon, emphasizing the need for scientific scrutiny and analysis.

5. Dr. Jane Goodall:

Dr. Jane Goodall, renowned for her groundbreaking work with chimpanzees, has expressed an open-minded perspective on the possibility of undiscovered hominids like Bigfoot. While not directly involved in Bigfoot research, her stature as a respected primatologist and her willingness to entertain the idea of unknown hominid species provide some credibility to the subject. Goodall's endorsement of keeping an open mind and supporting thorough investigations aligns with scientific principles.

While the scientific community as a whole maintains a skeptical stance toward Bigfoot, there have been notable scientists and researchers who have engaged in dedicated studies on the subject. Dr. Grover Krantz, Dr. Jeff Meldrum, Dr. John Bindernagel, Dr. Esteban Sarmiento, and Dr. Jane Goodall are among those who have contributed their scientific expertise and conducted rigorous investigations into the phenomenon. Their work has brought scientific scrutiny and methodologies to the study of Bigfoot, challenging the prevailing skepticism and fostering further exploration and discussion within the scientific community. Despite the ongoing debates, the contributions of these notable scientists and researchers have helped shape the field of Bigfoot studies and inspire continued scientific inquiry.

Chapter 7: Skepticism and Debunking Bigfoot

The existence of Bigfoot has long been a subject of skepticism and debate within the scientific community. While some researchers and enthusiasts believe in the creature's existence, there are several skeptical viewpoints and arguments that challenge the validity of Bigfoot as a real, undiscovered species. In this section, we will explore some of the key skeptical viewpoints and arguments against the existence of Bigfoot.

One of the primary skeptical arguments against the existence of Bigfoot is the lack of conclusive physical evidence. Despite numerous reports, sightings, and footprint casts, no verifiable remains, DNA samples, or unequivocal visual documentation have been presented. Skeptics argue that in an age of advanced technology and widespread documentation, the absence of compelling physical evidence is questionable. The lack of substantial proof raises doubts about the existence of a large, bipedal creature like Bigfoot.

Another skeptical viewpoint revolves around the limited reproducibility of evidence associated with Bigfoot. Many eyewitness accounts, footprint casts, photographs, and video footage remain isolated incidents without the ability to be replicated under controlled conditions. Skeptics argue that for a scientific claim to be considered valid, it must be supported by evidence that can be consistently reproduced and independently verified. The anecdotal nature of much of the evidence surrounding Bigfoot raises concerns about its reliability and validity.

Skeptics often point to the history of hoaxes and misinterpretations as a reason to doubt the existence of Bigfoot. Throughout the years, numerous fraudulent claims and intentionally fabricated evidence have been exposed, eroding confidence in the authenticity of reported sightings and evidence. Skeptics argue that hoaxes, combined with misidentifications of known animals or natural phenomena, contribute to the perpetuation of the Bigfoot myth and undermine the credibility of genuine research efforts.

Another skeptical argument against Bigfoot's existence is the lack of coherent and consistent descriptions across reported sightings. Descriptions of Bigfoot vary significantly in terms of size, appearance, behavior, and vocalizations. Skeptics argue that if Bigfoot were a real, distinct species, there should be a more consistent and reliable set of characteristics attributed to the creature. The wide range of descriptions raises questions about the reliability of eyewitness testimonies and the potential influence of cultural beliefs or individual biases.

Critics also argue that the existence of a large, undiscovered primate species like Bigfoot contradicts established scientific knowledge. The lack of ecological support, such as viable breeding populations and sustainable habitats, raises doubts about the creature's survival and its ability to remain undetected by scientists and wildlife experts. Skeptics contend that the absence of Bigfoot within the established framework of scientific knowledge and understanding diminishes its plausibility as a genuine species.

Skeptical viewpoints and arguments against the existence of Bigfoot challenge the validity of the creature as a real, undiscovered species. The lack of conclusive physical evidence, limited reproducibility of evidence, hoaxes and misinterpretations, lack of coherent descriptions, and incongruity with established scientific knowledge are often cited as reasons to doubt the existence of Bigfoot. While proponents of Bigfoot research counter these arguments with claims of ongoing investigations, cultural significance, and the potential for undiscovered species, the skepticism within the scientific community underscores the need for rigorous scientific scrutiny and verifiable evidence to establish the existence of such a creature.

The subject of Bigfoot is often shrouded in myths, misconceptions, and occasional hoaxes. These misunderstandings and deliberate fabrications contribute to the complexity and controversy surrounding the phenomenon. In this section, we will address some of the common misconceptions and hoaxes related to Bigfoot, aiming to separate fact from fiction and promote a more accurate understanding of the subject.

One common misconception is that Bigfoot is merely a mythological creature or a figment of folklore. While Bigfoot has deep roots in native legends and cultural narratives, many individuals genuinely believe in its existence and conduct scientific investigations to gather evidence. The debate lies in the interpretation of the evidence, not the dismissal of Bigfoot as a purely mythological entity. It is important to recognize the ongoing research and exploration surrounding Bigfoot, regardless of personal beliefs.

Another misconception is the assumption that Bigfoot represents a single, uniform species. However, proponents of Bigfoot research suggest that there may be regional variations, subspecies, or different undiscovered hominids collectively referred to as Bigfoot. The diversity of reported sightings, descriptions, and footprints supports the idea that there might not be a single homogenous species, but rather a range of related creatures yet to be scientifically documented.

Popular culture often portrays Bigfoot as a menacing and aggressive creature, ready to harm humans. However, there is no concrete evidence to suggest that Bigfoot poses a threat to human safety. Most reported encounters describe Bigfoot as elusive, shy, and more interested in avoiding human contact than engaging in aggressive behavior. It is essential to separate fictional portrayals from actual witness accounts and respect the potentially elusive nature of the creature.

One notable hoax related to Bigfoot is the case of the "Cottingley Fairies" photographs. Although not directly tied to Bigfoot, it serves as a cautionary tale in the realm of photographic evidence. In 1917, young cousins Elsie Wright and Frances Griffiths took a series of photographs featuring themselves with what appeared to be fairies. The images gained widespread attention and belief until they were revealed as a hoax in 1983. This hoax reminds us of the need for critical analysis and skepticism when evaluating photographic evidence related to Bigfoot or any other extraordinary claim.

Ray Wallace, a logger, is often associated with perpetuating hoaxes related to Bigfoot. In 1958, Wallace claimed to have discovered large footprints in Bluff Creek, California, igniting interest in Bigfoot research. However, after his death in 2002, his family revealed that Wallace had been responsible for creating many of the footprint casts himself. This revelation cast doubt on the authenticity of some of the early evidence associated with Bigfoot, reinforcing the need for rigorous scrutiny and verification of evidence.

It is a misconception to assume that Bigfoot researchers lack skepticism or critical thinking. In fact, many researchers within the Bigfoot community employ scientific methods, engage in peer review, and rigorously analyze evidence. Skepticism and critical analysis are integral to scientific inquiry and are present within the Bigfoot research community. While there may be varying levels of skepticism among individuals, the pursuit of scientific understanding remains central to many researchers' endeavors.

Addressing common misconceptions and hoaxes related to Bigfoot is crucial for fostering a more accurate understanding of the phenomenon. It is essential to recognize that while Bigfoot has its roots in legends and cultural folklore, it also attracts genuine scientific investigation and scrutiny. By separating fact from fiction, acknowledging the existence of hoaxes, and promoting critical thinking, we can engage in informed discussions and approach Bigfoot research with an objective and discerning mindset.

Chapter 8: Anthropology and Bigfoot

Bigfoot's potential connection to primatology and human evolution is a topic of speculation and debate within the field of Bigfoot research. While the scientific community remains skeptical of Bigfoot's existence, proponents suggest that the creature, if real, could offer insights into the study of primatology and human evolutionary history. In this section, we will explore some of the arguments and theories that propose a connection between Bigfoot and primatology, as well as its potential implications for our understanding of human evolution.

Supporters of Bigfoot's existence argue that if the creature is a real, undiscovered species, it could belong to a branch of hominids or primates closely related to humans. They suggest that Bigfoot may represent a relict population of an extinct hominid or a divergent evolutionary lineage that evolved alongside humans. Exploring the genetics, anatomy, and behavior of Bigfoot, if proven real, could provide insights into our shared ancestry and shed light on the diversity of hominid species that once existed.

One intriguing aspect of Bigfoot is its reported bipedalism, which is a defining characteristic of the human lineage. Supporters argue that if Bigfoot exhibits true bipedalism, it could provide valuable information on the evolution of bipedal locomotion in hominids. By studying its footprints, skeletal structure, and movement patterns, researchers may gain insights into the anatomical adaptations and biomechanics associated with bipedalism in our early ancestors. Understanding the locomotor capabilities of Bigfoot, if substantiated, could contribute to our knowledge of hominid evolution.

Reports of Bigfoot behavior often describe social interactions, vocalizations, and territoriality, resembling patterns observed in other primates. If confirmed, the study of Bigfoot's behavior could offer parallels to the social organization and communication systems of primates. Observing how Bigfoot interacts within its hypothetical population, if it exists, may provide insights into the social structure, mating behaviors, and intelligence of hominid species. Such comparative studies could contribute to our understanding of the evolution of complex social behaviors in primates, including humans.

Bigfoot is commonly associated with remote forested areas, often described as its preferred habitat. Researchers argue that studying the ecological niche and habitat requirements of Bigfoot, if substantiated, could provide insights into the environmental factors that influenced the distribution and survival of ancient hominids. Understanding Bigfoot's ecological interactions, diet, and habitat preferences may help reconstruct the paleoenvironmental context in which hominid species evolved and adapted.

If Bigfoot were proven to be a real and endangered species, it could have significant conservation implications. Recognition of Bigfoot as a distinct hominid or primate species would prompt efforts to protect its habitat and ensure its survival. Conservation initiatives aimed at preserving the habitat of Bigfoot could indirectly benefit other species and ecosystems in the areas it occupies. By expanding our understanding of hominid diversity and evolution, the hypothetical existence of Bigfoot could foster a deeper appreciation for the natural world and its interconnectedness.

While Bigfoot's connection to primatology and human evolution remains speculative, proponents suggest that studying the creature, if real, could offer valuable insights into our shared ancestry and the diversity of hominid species. The potential exploration of Bigfoot's genetics, anatomy, behavior, and habitat preferences could contribute to our understanding of hominid evolution, including bipedalism, social behavior, and ecological adaptations. While the scientific community demands verifiable evidence before fully engaging with these theories, the hypothetical existence of Bigfoot poses intriguing questions and encourages exploration within the broader context of primatology and human evolutionary studies.

The classification and evolutionary history of Bigfoot, if it were proven to be a real creature, remain subjects of speculation and debate within the field of Bigfoot research. While the scientific community awaits conclusive evidence, proponents have proposed various theories regarding Bigfoot's potential classification and its place within the broader evolutionary context. In this section, we will explore some of these theories, acknowledging that they are speculative in nature until supported by robust scientific evidence.

1. Gigantopithecus Theory:

One prominent theory suggests a connection between Bigfoot and Gigantopithecus, an extinct genus of ape that lived in Asia during the Pleistocene epoch. Gigantopithecus was a massive primate, believed to have stood up to 10 feet tall (3 meters) and weighing up to 1,200 pounds (540 kilograms). Proponents argue that if Bigfoot exists, it could be a descendant of this ancient ape. The theory suggests that Gigantopithecus might have migrated to North America via the Bering land bridge and evolved into the creature known as Bigfoot.

2. Hominid or Homo Heidelbergensis Descendant:

Another theory proposes that Bigfoot could be a descendant of an early human ancestor, such as Homo heidelbergensis or another divergent lineage. Homo heidelbergensis lived in Africa and Eurasia around 600,000 to 200,000 years ago and is considered an ancestral species to both Neanderthals and modern humans. Proponents argue that a relic population of this species might have survived in isolated regions and evolved into Bigfoot. This theory suggests that Bigfoot could be a hominid species with distinct anatomical and behavioral characteristics.

3. Hybridization with Native American Populations:

Some theories suggest that Bigfoot could be the result of ancient hybridization between early human populations and non-human hominid species. Proponents argue that interactions between Native American populations and other hominid species could have led to the emergence of Bigfoot.

BIGFOOT: THE COMPREHENSIVE INVESTIGATION INTO THE ELUSIVE LEGEND

This theory suggests that Bigfoot represents a unique genetic lineage resulting from interbreeding and adaptation to specific environmental conditions.

4. Unknown Primate Species:

An alternative theory proposes that Bigfoot is a completely unknown and undiscovered primate species, potentially belonging to a new genus within the primate family tree. Proponents argue that there might be hidden pockets of wilderness and remote regions where undiscovered primate species could still exist. This theory suggests that Bigfoot could be a highly adapted primate that has successfully evaded human detection.

5. Relict Hominid Population:

This theory posits that Bigfoot represents a relict population of an early hominid species, potentially surviving in isolated and unexplored regions. Proponents argue that if Bigfoot is real, it may be a relic species that avoided extinction and managed to survive through adaptive behaviors, elusive habits, and limited human interaction. This theory suggests that Bigfoot's evolutionary history might date back to a time when multiple hominid species coexisted.

Theories regarding Bigfoot's classification and evolutionary history are speculative and lack conclusive evidence. The Gigantopithecus theory, connection to Homo heidelbergensis or other early human ancestors, hybridization with Native American populations, existence as an unknown primate species, and relict hominid population are among the proposed explanations. However, until substantial evidence is obtained, these theories remain speculative in nature. The challenge lies in conducting rigorous scientific investigations, collecting verifiable evidence, and subjecting it to peer review and analysis. Only through such scientific scrutiny can the mysteries surrounding Bigfoot's classification and evolutionary history be truly unraveled.

Chapter 9: Genetics and DNA Analysis

In the quest to determine the existence of Bigfoot, various DNA studies have been conducted on alleged samples attributed to the creature. These studies aim to analyze the genetic material in order to identify potential links to known species or unveil novel genetic sequences. In this section, we will investigate some of the DNA studies conducted on alleged Bigfoot samples and explore their findings and implications.

1. The Sasquatch Genome Project (2012):

The Sasquatch Genome Project, led by Dr. Melba Ketchum, aimed to provide genetic evidence of Bigfoot's existence. This study involved the analysis of DNA samples collected from purported Bigfoot sources, such as hair, tissue, and other biological materials. The project claimed to have obtained novel mitochondrial DNA sequences and nuclear DNA sequences that did not match any known species. However, the project faced significant criticism from the scientific community for its methodology, lack of transparency, and limited peer-reviewed publication of results. As a result, the scientific consensus remains skeptical of the Sasquatch Genome Project's findings.

2. The Oxford-Lausanne Collateral Hominid Project (2014):

The Oxford-Lausanne Collateral Hominid Project, conducted by Professor Bryan Sykes, aimed to analyze DNA samples attributed to Bigfoot and other cryptid species. The project solicited samples from individuals claiming to possess Bigfoot hair or tissue. After conducting genetic analysis, the study found that all samples tested were from known animal species, such as bears, raccoons, and cows. The project concluded that no evidence of an unknown primate or hominid species, including Bigfoot, was detected in the analyzed samples.

3. The Erickson Project (2013):

The Erickson Project, led by Adrian Erickson, conducted DNA analysis on samples purportedly linked to Bigfoot. The project obtained hair samples, which were subjected to genetic testing. The results reportedly revealed unknown primate DNA, distinct from any known species. However, the study has faced criticism for its lack of transparency and scientific rigor. The findings have not been independently verified or published in peer-reviewed journals, leading to skepticism within the scientific community.

4. The Ketchum Report (2013):

The Ketchum Report, authored by Dr. Melba Ketchum, claimed to present comprehensive DNA analysis supporting the existence of Bigfoot. The report suggested that Bigfoot represented a novel species of hominin, possibly originating from hybridization events between humans and an unknown primate. However, the report was met with significant skepticism and criticism from the scientific community. The lack of publication in reputable scientific journals and the absence of independent verification have prevented the Ketchum Report's findings from gaining acceptance within the scientific community.

DNA studies conducted on alleged Bigfoot samples have been met with varying degrees of skepticism and controversy within the scientific community. The Sasquatch Genome Project, the Oxford-Lausanne Collateral Hominid Project, the Erickson Project, and the Ketchum Report represent some of the notable studies conducted. However, limitations such as questionable methodology, lack of transparency, and insufficient independent verification have cast doubt on the findings. The scientific community remains cautious and requires robust, peer-reviewed research that meets stringent scientific standards to establish the existence of Bigfoot through DNA analysis. Until such evidence is provided, the question of Bigfoot's existence remains open, and further scientific inquiry is necessary to unravel the mysteries surrounding this elusive creature.

Genetic evidence has been sought after as a means to provide definitive proof of Bigfoot's existence. DNA analysis holds the potential to shed light on the creature's identity, evolutionary relationships, and its place within the natural world. However, the validity and limitations of genetic evidence in the Bigfoot debate are subjects of ongoing scrutiny. In this section, we will analyze the strengths, weaknesses, and challenges associated with genetic evidence in the context of the Bigfoot debate.

1. Strengths of Genetic Evidence:

a) Species Identification: Genetic analysis can help identify the species to which a sample belongs. By comparing the DNA sequences with those of known species, researchers can determine if the sample belongs to a recognized species or potentially represents a novel species.

b) Phylogenetic Relationships: Genetic data can provide insights into the evolutionary relationships between different species. By comparing the DNA sequences of Bigfoot samples with those of closely related species, researchers can potentially determine the creature's place within the primate family tree.

c) Population Genetics: Genetic analysis can shed light on the population structure, genetic diversity, and potential breeding patterns of a species. This information can provide insights into Bigfoot's population dynamics and dispersal patterns, if it exists.

2. Limitations and Challenges of Genetic Evidence:

a) Sample Quality and Preservation: Obtaining high-quality DNA samples from alleged Bigfoot sources can be challenging. Factors such as degradation, contamination, and improper collection techniques can compromise the quality and integrity of the DNA. Obtaining viable DNA from hair, for example, can be particularly challenging, as hair lacks the nuclear DNA necessary for comprehensive analysis.

b) Lack of Baseline Data: Without baseline genetic data from confirmed Bigfoot individuals, it is challenging to establish a reference point for comparison. Without a reference sample, it becomes difficult to differentiate between potential contamination or sample mix-ups and genuine Bigfoot DNA.

c) Small Sample Size and Reproducibility: The number of samples available for analysis is often limited, and studies with small sample sizes can be prone to biased results or insufficient statistical power. Reproducibility, the ability to replicate results independently, is a cornerstone of scientific investigation, but limited access to Bigfoot samples hampers efforts to confirm and validate findings.

d) Lack of Standardized Protocols: The absence of standardized protocols for Bigfoot DNA analysis poses challenges. Varying methodologies, genetic markers, and interpretation frameworks across different studies can lead to inconsistencies and make it difficult to compare and evaluate results.

e) Contamination and Hoaxes: Contamination of samples, intentional hoaxes, and misidentification of known animal DNA can confound genetic analysis. The risk of contamination increases when handling low-quality or degraded samples, potentially leading to erroneous results.

3. Scientific Skepticism and Peer Review:

To establish the validity of genetic evidence, it is crucial to subject findings to rigorous scientific scrutiny and peer review. Skepticism within the scientific community is healthy and necessary to ensure that claims are supported by robust evidence and scientific standards. Peer review facilitates independent evaluation, verification, and replication of results, enhancing the credibility of genetic studies.

Genetic evidence holds promise as a means to provide insights into the identity and evolutionary relationships of Bigfoot. However, the validity and limitations of genetic evidence in the Bigfoot debate are significant. Challenges such as sample quality, lack of baseline data, small sample sizes, lack of standard protocols, and the potential for contamination and hoaxes present obstacles in obtaining reliable results. Scientific skepticism, rigorous peer review, and adherence to standardized methodologies are essential to establish the credibility and validity of genetic evidence in the context of the Bigfoot debate. Until robust, peer-reviewed genetic studies are conducted with appropriate sample sizes and stringent protocols, the role of genetic evidence in resolving the Bigfoot debate remains inconclusive.

Chapter 10: Bigfoot in Native American Legends

Native American mythology has a rich tradition of stories and beliefs surrounding mysterious creatures resembling Bigfoot. These legends and accounts provide cultural context and historical perspective to the phenomenon. In this section, we will explore the connection between Native American mythology and Bigfoot, examining the various tribes' beliefs, names, and interpretations of these creatures.

1. Tribal Beliefs and Legends:

Many Native American tribes have long-held beliefs in the existence of large, hairy, and elusive creatures similar to Bigfoot. These beings are often referred to by different names in different tribes. For example, the Lakota Sioux call them "Chiye-tanka," while the Algonquian tribes use names like "Windigo" or "Wendigo." Tribes such as the Salish, Chehalis, and Lummi have their own names for these creatures as well.

2. Protectors of the Forest:

In Native American mythology, Bigfoot-like creatures are often associated with the natural environment, particularly forests and mountains. They are believed to be guardians or protectors of the wilderness, possessing supernatural abilities and knowledge of the land. Tribes consider encounters with these creatures as both rare and sacred, with some viewing them as spiritual entities connected to the balance of nature.

3. Oral Traditions and Historical Accounts:

Native American oral traditions, passed down through generations, recount encounters with large, hairy creatures resembling Bigfoot. These stories often serve to explain natural phenomena or teach moral lessons. While specific details may vary between tribes, the overarching theme of a powerful, elusive, and semi-spiritual creature is prevalent in many accounts.

4. Cultural Significance and Respect:

Within Native American communities, Bigfoot-like creatures are regarded with respect and caution. Tribes approach encounters with reverence, emphasizing the need to coexist harmoniously with the natural world and showing respect for these powerful beings. Some tribes discourage seeking out or disturbing these creatures, as they are considered part of the spiritual fabric of the land.

5. Modern Interactions and Perspectives:

Contemporary Native American communities continue to hold diverse beliefs and perspectives regarding Bigfoot. Some individuals consider encounters with Bigfoot to be part of their cultural heritage and a validation of ancestral knowledge. Others approach Bigfoot as a subject of curiosity, cultural preservation, or spiritual connection. It is important to recognize and respect the range of beliefs and perspectives held by different tribes and individuals within Native American communities.

6. Influence on Bigfoot Research:

Native American mythology and accounts have had a significant impact on the field of Bigfoot research. Researchers have drawn inspiration from Native American stories, incorporating cultural perspectives and historical knowledge into their investigations. Collaborative efforts between researchers and Native American communities seek to bridge scientific inquiry with traditional beliefs, fostering cultural preservation and mutual understanding.

Native American mythology contributes valuable cultural context and historical perspective to the phenomenon of Bigfoot. The beliefs, legends, and encounters recounted within Native American communities provide a unique lens through which to understand and appreciate the significance of Bigfoot-like creatures. Their connection to the natural world, spiritual significance, and role as protectors of the wilderness offer insights into the complex relationship between indigenous cultures and the environment. By acknowledging and respecting Native American perspectives, researchers can gain a more holistic understanding of Bigfoot and foster collaborative approaches that blend scientific inquiry with cultural preservation.

Bigfoot, or similar hairy and elusive creatures, holds significant cultural and spiritual significance in various indigenous cultures around the world. These creatures are often deeply woven into the fabric of indigenous beliefs, stories, and traditions. In this section, we will explore the significance of Bigfoot in indigenous cultures, focusing on its role in spirituality, ecological stewardship, cultural identity, and the preservation of traditional knowledge.

In many indigenous cultures, Bigfoot-like creatures are regarded as supernatural beings or spirit entities. They are believed to possess unique powers, wisdom, and connections to the spiritual realm. Indigenous communities often view encounters with these creatures as transformative experiences, leading to spiritual awakenings, visions, or insights. Bigfoot is seen as an intermediary between the human and spirit worlds, bridging the gap between the material and the divine.

Bigfoot is frequently associated with the natural environment, particularly forests, mountains, and remote wilderness areas. Indigenous cultures consider these creatures as guardians or protectors of the land. They are seen as embodiment of the wilderness, symbolizing the delicate balance between humans and nature. Indigenous communities view Bigfoot as a reminder of the importance of ecological stewardship, sustainable resource management, and maintaining a harmonious relationship with the natural world.

Bigfoot holds a special place in the cultural identity of many indigenous communities. These creatures are often deeply embedded in oral traditions, legends, and historical accounts passed down through generations. The stories surrounding Bigfoot serve as a means to preserve cultural heritage, transmit traditional knowledge, and reinforce communal values.

BIGFOOT: THE COMPREHENSIVE INVESTIGATION INTO THE ELUSIVE LEGEND

Bigfoot's significance is rooted in the connection to ancestral wisdom, shaping indigenous identities and strengthening cultural bonds.

Indigenous cultures often interpret encounters with Bigfoot as lessons in ecological awareness and respect for the environment. These creatures are seen as indicators of environmental health and indicators of the well-being of the land. The presence or absence of Bigfoot is believed to reflect the state of balance and harmony within ecosystems. Indigenous communities use the stories of Bigfoot as teaching tools to pass down ecological wisdom, emphasizing the importance of sustainable practices and coexistence with nature.

In some indigenous cultures, Bigfoot is associated with healing and medicine. The creatures are believed to possess knowledge of medicinal plants, spiritual remedies, and healing practices. Indigenous healers may seek guidance from Bigfoot through rituals, visions, or dreams. The belief in the healing powers of Bigfoot reinforces the connection between spiritual well-being, physical health, and the natural world.

Bigfoot and similar creatures have also been invoked in indigenous activism and movements for sovereignty and self-determination. They symbolize the resistance against colonization, the preservation of indigenous lands and resources, and the protection of cultural traditions. The figure of Bigfoot represents the resilience, strength, and ongoing struggle for indigenous rights and the reclamation of ancestral territories.

The significance of Bigfoot in indigenous cultures extends beyond mere folklore or myth. It plays a vital role in spirituality, ecological stewardship, cultural identity, and the preservation of traditional knowledge. Bigfoot serves as a bridge between the human and spiritual realms, a symbol of ecological balance, and a repository of ancestral wisdom. Understanding and respecting the significance of Bigfoot in indigenous cultures is crucial for building collaborative relationships, acknowledging indigenous perspectives, and appreciating the profound connections between humans, nature, and the spiritual world.

Chapter 11: Bigfoot in Popular Culture

Bigfoot, with its intriguing folklore and elusive nature, has captured the imagination of people worldwide, leading to its portrayal in various forms of media. From movies to literature and other forms of popular culture, Bigfoot has become a popular subject, often depicted in diverse and sometimes sensationalized ways. In this section, we will trace the portrayal of Bigfoot in movies, literature, and media, exploring its evolving image and influence on popular culture.

1. Early Depictions:

a) Movies: In the early days of cinema, Bigfoot made appearances in low-budget horror films like "The Legend of Boggy Creek" (1972) and "Creature from Black Lake" (1976). These movies portrayed Bigfoot as a menacing creature terrorizing rural communities, capitalizing on the fear of the unknown.

b) Literature: Bigfoot found its way into various books, often categorized as cryptozoology or paranormal literature. These works blended legends, eyewitness accounts, and speculative fiction to create compelling narratives around the creature's existence, adventures, and encounters with humans.

2. Popularity and Expansion:

a) Movies: The popularity of Bigfoot grew in the 1980s and 1990s, leading to the release of movies such as "Harry and the Hendersons" (1987). This family-friendly film presented Bigfoot in a more sympathetic light, depicting a friendly, intelligent, and lovable creature who forms a bond with humans.

b) Television: Bigfoot became a recurring theme in television shows, appearing in episodes of popular series like "The Six Million Dollar Man," "The X-Files," and "Supernatural." These portrayals often incorporated elements of mystery, conspiracy, and the search for the truth.

c) Literature: Bigfoot-inspired literature expanded, with authors exploring the creature's mythology, origins, and cultural significance. Some works blended Bigfoot with other cryptids or paranormal elements, while others focused on exploring the psychological and emotional aspects of encountering such a mysterious creature.

3. Parodies and Comedic Portrayals:

a) Movies: Bigfoot became a subject of parody and comedic portrayals, appearing in films like "Bigfoot: The Unforgettable Encounter" (1994) and "Bigfoot vs. D.B. Cooper" (2014). These films used humor to play with the mythos surrounding Bigfoot, often presenting humorous or absurd scenarios.

b) Television: Bigfoot parodies and comedic portrayals also made their way into television shows, with animated series like "South Park" featuring episodes centered around the creature. These portrayals used satire and comedy to comment on various aspects of Bigfoot mythology and pop culture fascination.

4. Cryptozoology and Documentary Approaches:

a) Documentaries: As interest in cryptozoology and unexplained phenomena grew, documentaries started exploring the subject of Bigfoot more seriously. Documentaries like "Sasquatch: Legend Meets Science" (2003) and "Discovering Bigfoot" (2017) aimed to provide scientific investigation, interviews, and analysis of alleged evidence related to Bigfoot.

b) Reality Television: Bigfoot hunting and investigation became the focus of reality television shows such as "Finding Bigfoot" and "Mountain Monsters." These programs followed teams of researchers and enthusiasts as they searched for evidence, interviewed witnesses, and explored areas known for Bigfoot sightings.

5. Modern Portrayals and Cultural Impact:

a) Movies and Television: Bigfoot continues to make appearances in contemporary movies and television series. Some films, like "Willow Creek" (2013) and "Primal Rage" (2018), explore horror and suspense elements, while others, such as the animated film "Smallfoot" (2018), provide a light-hearted and imaginative take on Bigfoot mythology.

b) Internet and Social Media: Bigfoot's presence has expanded on the internet and social media platforms, with online communities dedicated to discussing sightings, sharing stories, and analyzing alleged evidence. The rise of video-sharing platforms has allowed for the dissemination of purported Bigfoot footage, contributing to its continued presence in popular culture.

The portrayal of Bigfoot in movies, literature, and media has evolved over time, reflecting changing societal perceptions, cultural fascination, and the blending of fact and fiction. From early horror films to family-friendly movies and comedic parodies, Bigfoot has become an enduring figure in popular culture. Additionally, the rise of documentaries, reality television, and online communities has expanded the exploration of Bigfoot and its cultural impact. Through these portrayals, Bigfoot has become a symbol of mystery, exploration, and the enduring human fascination with the unknown.

Bigfoot, with its enigmatic nature and widespread legends, has left an indelible mark on popular culture. The creature's enduring appeal can be attributed to its mystique, the intrigue surrounding its existence, and its ability to tap into the human fascination with the unknown. In this section, we will examine the influence of Bigfoot on popular culture and explore the factors that contribute to its enduring appeal.

1. Folklore and Urban Legends:

Bigfoot's influence on popular culture can be traced back to its origins in Native American folklore and regional urban legends. These stories, passed down through generations, have captivated imaginations and sparked curiosity. The enduring appeal of Bigfoot lies in its connection to ancient legends and the power of storytelling, perpetuating its mystique and adding to its allure.

2. Cryptid Culture and Cryptozoology:

Bigfoot is one of the most prominent cryptids, creatures that are rumored or believed to exist but lack scientific confirmation. The field of cryptozoology, which investigates and studies such elusive creatures, has given Bigfoot a platform for exploration and debate. The allure of searching for hidden creatures and the hope of discovering a new species adds excitement and adventure to the cultural fascination with Bigfoot.

3. Entertainment and Media:

Bigfoot has become a popular subject in various forms of entertainment and media. It has appeared in movies, television shows, documentaries, literature, and even video games. These portrayals cater to diverse audiences, ranging from horror enthusiasts to families seeking adventure and humor. Bigfoot's presence in popular culture offers a mix of suspense, mystery, and a touch of the supernatural, providing entertainment and escapism for audiences.

4. Merchandising and Iconic Imagery:

The iconic image of Bigfoot, often depicted as a large, hairy creature with distinct footprints, has become ingrained in popular culture. This imagery has been utilized in merchandise, including t-shirts, toys, posters, and other memorabilia, capitalizing on the creature's recognition and popularity. The ability to wear or own items featuring Bigfoot contributes to its cultural influence and serves as a conversation starter or symbol of intrigue.

5. Cultural and Social Identity:

Bigfoot has been embraced by certain subcultures and communities, who identify with its mystique and its representation of wilderness and adventure. It has become a symbol of regional pride for areas known for Bigfoot sightings, fostering a sense of shared identity and community. Additionally, Bigfoot's enduring appeal intersects with environmentalism, as it represents a connection to nature and the importance of ecological conservation.

6. Human Fascination with the Unknown:

The enduring appeal of Bigfoot can be attributed to humanity's innate fascination with the unknown and the unexplained. Bigfoot embodies the mystery and wonder that captivate our imagination and push the boundaries of our understanding. Its existence, or the possibility thereof, challenges our perception of the natural world and our place within it, inspiring exploration and a sense of awe.

Bigfoot's influence on popular culture is undeniable, with its enduring appeal rooted in folklore, cryptid culture, entertainment, merchandising, and the human fascination with the unknown. Its presence in movies, literature, and media provides entertainment, intrigue, and a platform for exploration and debate. Bigfoot has become a symbol of mystery, adventure, and the enduring human desire to seek answers to unexplained phenomena. As long as the allure of the unknown persists, Bigfoot will continue to capture the imagination and hold its place in popular culture.

Chapter 12: Bigfoot Tourism and Local Legends

Bigfoot, with its wide-ranging legends and alleged sightings, has led to the emergence of several regions that have become renowned for their association with the creature. These areas attract enthusiasts, researchers, and tourists seeking to explore the mysteries surrounding Bigfoot. In this section, we will investigate some of the regions renowned for Bigfoot sightings and the associated tourism they have generated.

1. Pacific Northwest, United States:

The Pacific Northwest, particularly the states of Washington, Oregon, and northern California, is often considered the epicenter of Bigfoot sightings and research. This region is known for its vast forests, remote wilderness areas, and rugged terrain, creating an ideal habitat for an elusive creature. Locations like the dense forests of the Olympic Peninsula, the Cascade Mountains, and the Pacific Coast have reported numerous alleged Bigfoot encounters, contributing to the region's reputation as a hotspot for Bigfoot activity. The towns of Willow Creek (California) and Forks (Washington) have embraced their connections to Bigfoot, establishing museums, annual festivals, and guided tours that cater to Bigfoot enthusiasts and tourists.

2. British Columbia, Canada:

British Columbia, situated in the westernmost part of Canada, is another prominent region associated with Bigfoot sightings. The province's vast wilderness, including its expansive forests and rugged mountains, offers potential habitats for Bigfoot-like creatures. Areas such as Harrison Hot Springs and the Fraser River Valley have reported a significant number of alleged encounters and have become focal points for Bigfoot research. The region attracts researchers, enthusiasts, and tourists interested in exploring the rugged landscapes and investigating the mysteries of Bigfoot.

3. The Four Corners Region, United States:

The Four Corners region, where the states of Arizona, New Mexico, Colorado, and Utah meet, has also gained attention as a Bigfoot sighting hotspot. This area is characterized by diverse landscapes, including desert regions, mountain ranges, and dense forests. Locations such as the San Juan Mountains and the Navajo Nation have reported Bigfoot sightings, sparking interest from researchers and tourists alike. The region's unique blend of Native American culture, folklore, and the potential for Bigfoot encounters adds to its allure as a destination for Bigfoot enthusiasts.

4. Southeastern United States:

While the Pacific Northwest dominates the Bigfoot narrative, the southeastern United States has its own share of alleged sightings and legends. The region's dense forests, swamplands, and rural areas provide a habitat conducive to the survival of an elusive creature. States such as Florida, Georgia, and Arkansas have reported sightings and fostered interest in Bigfoot research. The town of Falkville, Alabama gained attention in the 1970s for the "Falkville Monster" sighting, contributing to the region's reputation as an area of Bigfoot activity.

5. International Locations:

Bigfoot-like creatures are not limited to North America, as sightings and legends exist in other parts of the world. For example, the Himalayan region has its own version of Bigfoot known as the Yeti or Abominable Snowman. Locations like the Everest region in Nepal, Bhutan, and the Tibetan Plateau have drawn interest from adventurers and researchers seeking evidence of these elusive creatures. Additionally, Australia has its own version known as the Yowie, with reported sightings primarily in remote areas and national parks.

Associated Tourism:

The popularity of Bigfoot legends and alleged sightings has led to the development of associated tourism in these regions. Local businesses cater to Bigfoot enthusiasts, offering guided tours, museum exhibits, gift shops, and annual festivals dedicated to the creature. Visitors can explore Bigfoot-themed trails, attend lectures and conferences by researchers, participate in night vigils, or join expeditions to search for evidence of Bigfoot. These tourism initiatives generate economic opportunities for local communities and provide an immersive experience for those interested in the mysteries of Bigfoot.

Regions renowned for Bigfoot sightings have become hubs for enthusiasts, researchers, and tourists interested in exploring the legends and mysteries surrounding the creature. The Pacific Northwest, British Columbia, the Four Corners region, and the southeastern United States have all gained recognition for their association with Bigfoot sightings. These areas provide unique landscapes, diverse ecosystems, and cultural contexts that contribute to the allure and fascination with Bigfoot. The associated tourism, including guided tours, museums, and festivals, provides opportunities for visitors to engage with the legend, explore the wilderness, and immerse themselves in the mysteries of Bigfoot.

Communities renowned for Bigfoot sightings and associated tourism have embraced their connections to the creature by developing local folklore, hosting festivals, and creating attractions that celebrate the legend. These efforts provide an avenue for locals and visitors alike to immerse themselves in the mysteries and folklore surrounding Bigfoot. In this section, we will highlight some examples of local folklore, festivals, and attractions related to Bigfoot in various regions.

1. Willow Creek Bigfoot Days, California, USA:

Willow Creek, a town in California's Humboldt County, is known as the "Bigfoot capital of the world" and hosts the annual Willow Creek Bigfoot Days festival. This event brings together enthusiasts, researchers, and curious visitors for a weekend of activities that celebrate Bigfoot. The festival includes lectures, guest speakers, film screenings, art exhibits, guided hikes, and vendor booths offering Bigfoot-themed merchandise. Attendees can explore the town's Bigfoot Museum and participate in the Bigfoot parade, immersing themselves in the local folklore and embracing the spirit of the legend.

2. Sasquatch Summit, Washington, USA:

The Sasquatch Summit takes place in Ocean Shores, Washington, and is a gathering that focuses on all things Bigfoot. The event features presentations by researchers, eyewitnesses, and experts in the field of Bigfoot research. Attendees have the opportunity to listen to compelling stories, engage in discussions, and participate in field investigations. The summit provides a platform for sharing knowledge, fostering community, and promoting the exploration of the Bigfoot phenomenon.

3. Harrison Hot Springs Sasquatch Days, British Columbia, Canada:

Harrison Hot Springs, a picturesque community in British Columbia, hosts the Sasquatch Days festival. This event combines indigenous traditions, cultural celebrations, and the legend of Bigfoot. Visitors can enjoy live music, storytelling, First Nations dance performances, traditional food, and arts and crafts. The festival offers a unique blend of local folklore, indigenous heritage, and the spirit of Bigfoot, creating an immersive experience that showcases the cultural richness of the region.

4. International Cryptozoology Museum, Maine, USA:

Located in Portland, Maine, the International Cryptozoology Museum is dedicated to the study and exploration of elusive and undiscovered creatures, including Bigfoot. The museum features exhibits showcasing cryptozoological artifacts, evidence, and artwork. Visitors can learn about various cryptids, including Bigfoot, through educational displays and presentations. The museum serves as a hub for cryptozoology enthusiasts, researchers, and those curious about the mysteries of the natural world.

5. Skamania County Chamber of Commerce, Washington, USA:

Skamania County, Washington, has embraced its association with Bigfoot by creating the "Sasquatch Refuge" and the "Sasquatch Ordinance." The county recognizes Bigfoot as an important part of its cultural heritage and seeks to protect the creature's habitat. Visitors can explore the Sasquatch Refuge, which offers hiking trails and scenic vistas, and learn about the local legends and folklore. The Sasquatch Ordinance encourages the responsible pursuit of evidence and acknowledges the potential economic impact of Bigfoot-related tourism.

6. Bigfoot Discovery Museum, California, USA:

Located in Felton, California, the Bigfoot Discovery Museum is a small, volunteer-run institution dedicated to the study and documentation of Bigfoot. The museum features exhibits showcasing plaster casts of alleged Bigfoot footprints, photographs, maps, and a collection of Bigfoot-related artifacts. Visitors can engage with the local folklore, learn about notable sightings, and explore the ongoing research surrounding Bigfoot.

Communities associated with Bigfoot sightings have capitalized on their connections to the legend by creating local folklore, hosting festivals, and developing attractions that celebrate Bigfoot. Events such as the Willow Creek Bigfoot Days, Sasquatch Summit, and Harrison Hot Springs Sasquatch Days provide platforms for enthusiasts, researchers, and locals to engage with the legends and mysteries surrounding Bigfoot. Museums like the International Cryptozoology Museum and the Bigfoot Discovery Museum offer educational experiences that delve into the realm of cryptozoology. These efforts not only provide entertainment and tourism opportunities but also serve as a means to preserve local folklore, share knowledge, and foster a sense of community. By embracing the spirit of Bigfoot, these communities create immersive experiences that captivate the imagination and invite visitors to explore the legends and mysteries surrounding the creature.

Chapter 13: Bigfoot Hotspots

While Bigfoot sightings and activity are often reported across various regions, there are several areas that have gained a reputation for frequent encounters or a higher concentration of alleged sightings. It is important to note that the authenticity of these sightings is a subject of debate and scientific investigation. Here are some areas that have been associated with frequent Bigfoot sightings and activity:

1. Pacific Northwest, United States:

- Washington: Regions such as the Olympic Peninsula, Gifford Pinchot National Forest, and Mount St. Helens have reported numerous alleged Bigfoot sightings.

- Oregon: Areas like the Mount Hood National Forest, Willamette National Forest, and the southern Cascades have had reported sightings and encounters.

- Northern California: Locations such as the Six Rivers National Forest, Trinity Alps, and the Marble Mountain Wilderness have been associated with alleged Bigfoot activity.

2. British Columbia, Canada:

- Regions in British Columbia, including Harrison Hot Springs, the Fraser River Valley, and the wilderness areas of Vancouver Island, have reported numerous Bigfoot sightings and encounters.

3. Ohio, United States:

- The southeastern part of Ohio, specifically the Wayne National Forest and the Appalachian foothills, has gained a reputation for frequent Bigfoot sightings, leading to the area being referred to as the "Ohio Grassman" hotspot.

4. Florida, United States:

- The Florida Everglades and the remote swamplands of the state have seen reports of Bigfoot-like creatures known as the "Skunk Ape."

5. Arkansas, United States:

- The Fouke area, including Boggy Creek and the surrounding swamplands, gained attention in the 1970s due to reports of the "Fouke Monster" or "Boggy Creek Monster."

6. Appalachian Mountains, United States:

- The Appalachian Mountains, spanning multiple states including West Virginia, Tennessee, and Kentucky, have had various reports of Bigfoot-like creatures. The dense forests and remote regions of these mountains provide potential habitats for such elusive creatures.

7. Himalayan Region:

- The Himalayan region, including Nepal, Bhutan, and Tibet, is associated with sightings of a similar creature known as the Yeti or Abominable Snowman.

BIGFOOT: THE COMPREHENSIVE INVESTIGATION INTO THE ELUSIVE LEGEND

It's important to remember that the frequency and credibility of Bigfoot sightings in these areas vary, and the scientific community remains divided on the existence of the creature. Reports of Bigfoot sightings are often anecdotal and lack scientific verification. However, these regions have become known for alleged encounters and attract enthusiasts, researchers, and tourists interested in exploring the legends and mysteries surrounding Bigfoot.

The potential existence of Bigfoot raises questions about the geological and environmental factors that could support the presence of such a creature. While the existence of Bigfoot is still debated, exploring the geological and environmental aspects can provide insights into the hypothetical conditions that might contribute to its survival. In this section, we will examine some of the factors that have been theorized to play a role in supporting Bigfoot's potential presence.

1. Dense Forests and Remote Wilderness Areas:

Bigfoot sightings often occur in regions characterized by dense forests and remote wilderness areas. These areas provide ample cover and limited human presence, creating an environment where a large, elusive creature could potentially remain hidden. Dense vegetation, such as old-growth forests or extensive woodlands, can provide suitable habitat and resources for survival, including food sources and shelter.

2. Mountainous and Rugged Terrain:

Mountainous and rugged terrains are often associated with reported Bigfoot sightings. These regions offer various advantages for an elusive creature, including secluded valleys, deep canyons, and inaccessible areas that provide natural barriers and limited human access. The steep slopes, rocky outcrops, and dense vegetation in mountainous regions can provide suitable habitats and cover for a large creature like Bigfoot.

3. Abundance of Water Sources:

Bigfoot sightings have been reported near water sources, such as rivers, lakes, and streams. These water bodies provide essential resources for survival, including drinking water and potential food sources like fish or other aquatic life. Moreover, water sources attract a diverse range of wildlife, which could serve as a food supply for a large, omnivorous creature like Bigfoot.

4. Extensive Cave Systems:

Some theories suggest that Bigfoot may utilize extensive cave systems for shelter and protection. Caves provide a natural refuge from extreme weather conditions, potential predators, and human interference. The presence of large cave systems within suitable habitats could offer potential hiding places and provide a secure environment for Bigfoot.

5. Limited Human Encroachment:

Bigfoot sightings often occur in areas with limited human encroachment, such as remote wilderness regions or protected natural areas. These areas may have lower human populations, limited infrastructure, or legal restrictions on access, reducing the likelihood of frequent encounters with humans and increasing the chances of an elusive creature like Bigfoot remaining undetected.

6. Biodiversity and Ecological Balance:

Regions with high biodiversity and ecological balance may provide more favorable conditions for a potential large creature like Bigfoot. Such areas would offer abundant food sources, including plant life, small animals, and potentially larger prey. The presence of a diverse range of species indicates a healthy ecosystem, which could support the existence of an apex predator like Bigfoot.

While the existence of Bigfoot is yet to be scientifically validated, exploring the geological and environmental factors that may contribute to its hypothetical presence can provide insights into the conditions that could support such a creature. Dense forests, remote wilderness areas, mountainous terrains, abundant water sources, extensive cave systems, limited human encroachment, and ecological balance are factors that have been theorized to play a role in supporting Bigfoot's potential survival. It is important to note that these factors are speculative and based on anecdotal evidence, as the existence of Bigfoot remains a subject of debate. Further scientific investigation, including ecological studies and comprehensive field research, would be necessary to provide a more conclusive understanding of Bigfoot's hypothetical presence and its ecological requirements.

Chapter 14: Modern Technological Advances

Advancements in technology have greatly enhanced the tools and methods available to researchers and enthusiasts investigating the elusive creature known as Bigfoot. Modern technology, such as drones and thermal imaging, has opened up new possibilities for gathering evidence, conducting field research, and analyzing potential sightings. In this section, we will discuss how these technological advancements aid Bigfoot research and contribute to the ongoing investigation of this mysterious creature.

1. Aerial Surveillance with Drones:

Drones, also known as unmanned aerial vehicles (UAVs), have revolutionized Bigfoot research by providing an aerial perspective of the terrain and allowing researchers to survey large areas efficiently. Drones equipped with high-resolution cameras can capture detailed aerial imagery and video footage, which can be analyzed for potential signs of Bigfoot activity, such as footprints, nest-like structures, or movement in dense vegetation. Aerial surveillance with drones allows researchers to access rugged or inaccessible terrain, monitor areas of interest, and expand the scope of their investigations.

2. Thermal Imaging Technology:

Thermal imaging cameras have proven to be valuable tools in Bigfoot research, particularly during nighttime investigations. These cameras detect heat signatures emitted by objects and living beings, creating a visual representation of temperature variations. Thermal imaging technology can help researchers identify potential heat signatures that may indicate the presence of a large creature moving through the environment, even in challenging lighting conditions or dense vegetation. By capturing thermal footage, researchers can gather data that may support or refute claims of Bigfoot sightings and aid in the documentation of potential encounters.

3. Audio Recording and Analysis:

Advancements in audio recording technology have allowed researchers to capture and analyze potential vocalizations attributed to Bigfoot. Digital audio recorders with sensitive microphones can be strategically placed in areas known for Bigfoot activity or in response to reported vocalizations. These recordings can capture sounds that are beyond the range of human hearing or distinguish subtle vocalizations from ambient noise. By analyzing the audio recordings, researchers can identify unique vocalizations, patterns, or possible communication among individuals, providing additional evidence for the presence of Bigfoot.

4. GPS Tracking and Mapping:

GPS (Global Positioning System) technology has become an essential tool for documenting and mapping Bigfoot sightings, encounters, and potential habitat areas. Researchers can use

GPS devices to precisely record the location of reported sightings or the discovery of potential evidence, such as footprints or scat. Mapping these data points creates a visual representation of Bigfoot-related activities, enabling researchers to identify potential hotspots, movement patterns, or areas that require further investigation. GPS technology also assists in data sharing and collaboration among researchers, contributing to a more comprehensive understanding of Bigfoot distribution and movement.

5. Image and Video Analysis:

Advancements in image and video analysis software have improved the scrutiny of visual evidence related to Bigfoot. Researchers can employ sophisticated algorithms and techniques to enhance and analyze images or videos captured during potential sightings. This includes the ability to stabilize shaky footage, enhance image clarity, analyze subject proportions and movements, and identify potential anomalies or objects of interest. These analytical tools contribute to a more objective and detailed examination of visual evidence, aiding in the identification of potential hoaxes or the identification of credible encounters.

Modern technology, including drones, thermal imaging cameras, audio recording devices, GPS tracking, and image analysis software, has significantly advanced Bigfoot research. These tools provide researchers with increased mobility, access to rugged terrain, improved visual and audio documentation capabilities, and enhanced analytical techniques. While technology cannot definitively prove or disprove the existence of Bigfoot, it plays a crucial role in the scientific investigation, documentation, and analysis of potential evidence. By leveraging these advancements, researchers and enthusiasts can collect data, conduct more comprehensive field research, and contribute to the ongoing exploration of the mysteries surrounding Bigfoot.

As Bigfoot research evolves, advancements in data collection and analysis techniques have played a vital role in improving the scientific rigor and objectivity of investigations. These advancements enable researchers to gather more precise and comprehensive data, analyze evidence with greater accuracy, and contribute to a more systematic understanding of the phenomenon. In this section, we will explore some of the notable advancements in data collection and analysis techniques that have influenced Bigfoot research.

1. Footprint Documentation and Analysis:

a) Three-Dimensional (3D) Scanning: Traditional methods of footprint documentation have been enhanced by 3D scanning technology. Specialized scanners create precise digital models of footprints, capturing fine details such as dermal ridges and pressure points. This enables researchers to create accurate replicas for further study and analysis.

b) Comparative Footprint Databases: Advances in database technology have facilitated the creation of comprehensive comparative footprint databases. Researchers can compare and match collected footprints against existing records to identify potential matches or similarities, allowing for a more systematic evaluation of footprint evidence.

2. DNA Sampling and Analysis:

a) Non-Invasive DNA Sampling: Non-invasive DNA sampling techniques, such as hair collection, scat analysis, or environmental DNA (eDNA) sampling, have advanced the field of genetic research in Bigfoot investigations. These methods allow researchers to collect potential DNA samples without direct contact with the creature, increasing the chances of obtaining viable genetic material for analysis.

b) Next-Generation Sequencing: Next-generation sequencing technologies have revolutionized genetic analysis by allowing for high-throughput sequencing of DNA samples. This technique enables researchers to obtain more detailed genetic information, analyze multiple samples simultaneously, and identify potential genetic markers specific to Bigfoot or other cryptid species.

3. Audio Analysis:

a) Acoustic Pattern Recognition: Advancements in acoustic pattern recognition software enable researchers to analyze audio recordings for potential vocalizations or other sounds associated with Bigfoot. These algorithms can help identify distinct vocal patterns, differentiate between natural and human-made sounds, and assist in the classification of recorded audio data.

b) Spectrogram Analysis: Spectrogram analysis provides a visual representation of sound frequencies over time. Researchers can examine spectrograms of audio recordings to identify unique vocalizations, measure their duration, pitch, and amplitude, and compare them to known animal vocalizations or human speech patterns.

4. Statistical Analysis and Pattern Recognition:

a) Data Mining and Machine Learning: Data mining and machine learning techniques allow researchers to analyze large datasets, identify patterns, and extract meaningful information. These approaches can be applied to Bigfoot research by analyzing various data points, such as sighting reports, environmental variables, and witness descriptions, to identify potential correlations or patterns that may shed light on Bigfoot behavior or distribution.

b) Geographic Information Systems (GIS): GIS technology enables researchers to integrate and analyze diverse geospatial data, including sighting locations, habitat characteristics, and environmental factors. GIS can help identify spatial patterns, evaluate habitat suitability, and create predictive models to determine potential Bigfoot activity hotspots or movement patterns.

Advancements in data collection and analysis techniques have transformed Bigfoot research, providing researchers with powerful tools to gather and evaluate evidence systematically. From footprint documentation and DNA analysis to audio recording analysis and statistical modeling, these advancements enable researchers to approach the investigation in a more rigorous and objective manner. By integrating modern technologies and methodologies, researchers can collect high-quality data, identify patterns, and contribute to a growing body of scientific knowledge surrounding the Bigfoot phenomenon. Continued advancements in data collection and analysis techniques will undoubtedly play a crucial role in future Bigfoot research, supporting efforts to uncover the truth behind this enduring mystery.

Chapter 15: Witness Testimonies and Personal Encounters

Firsthand accounts from individuals who claim to have encountered Bigfoot provide personal testimonies that contribute to the lore and ongoing investigation of this elusive creature. While it is important to approach these accounts with critical thinking, they offer insights into the experiences and perceptions of those who believe they have encountered Bigfoot. Here are a few examples of firsthand accounts:

1. Albert Ostman's Encounter (1924):

In 1924, Albert Ostman, a Canadian prospector, claimed to have been abducted and held captive by a family of Bigfoot for several days. According to his account, while camping near Toba Inlet, British Columbia, he was unexpectedly lifted from his tent and carried away by a male Bigfoot. Ostman described being taken to a cave where he encountered four Bigfoot individuals, including an adult male, female, and two juveniles. He managed to escape after several days when the Bigfoot relaxed their vigilance. Ostman's account gained attention and remains one of the most well-known and controversial Bigfoot abduction stories.

2. The Ape Canyon Incident (1924):

The Ape Canyon Incident is a famous encounter reported by a group of miners near Mount St. Helens in Washington state.

According to their account, they claimed to have been attacked by a group of Bigfoot creatures at their remote cabin in the summer of 1924. The miners alleged that the Bigfoot pounded on the cabin, threw rocks, and tried to break in, resulting in a night of fear and desperation. This account, along with accompanying footprints and alleged photographs, fueled speculation and interest in Bigfoot.

3. The Patterson-Gimlin Film (1967):

One of the most iconic pieces of Bigfoot evidence is the Patterson-Gimlin film. In 1967, Roger Patterson and Bob Gimlin captured a short video clip of a large, bipedal creature walking through a forested area in Bluff Creek, California. Patterson and Gimlin claimed to have encountered the creature while on a horseback expedition. The film, known as the Patterson-Gimlin film or simply the "PGF," continues to be analyzed and debated by experts and enthusiasts, with skeptics questioning its authenticity and proponents arguing for its credibility.

4. Sierra Sounds Recordings (1970s):

In the 1970s, Ron Morehead and Al Berry claimed to have recorded a series of vocalizations attributed to Bigfoot in the Sierra Nevada Mountains of California. The recordings, known as the "Sierra Sounds," captured a range of vocalizations, including whistles, screams, and alleged Bigfoot speech-like vocalizations. Morehead and Berry's account and the accompanying audio recordings have sparked curiosity and debate within the Bigfoot research community.

5. Contemporary Eyewitness Accounts:

Numerous contemporary eyewitness accounts of Bigfoot encounters continue to be reported. These accounts range from sightings in remote wilderness areas to close encounters with vocalizations and purported interactions with Bigfoot individuals. While individual experiences may vary, the consistency in descriptions of a large, bipedal creature with specific physical features, such as height, hair color, and distinct footprints, has been noted among some accounts.

It is important to note that firsthand accounts are subjective and can vary in credibility and detail. Skeptics argue that many encounters may be misidentifications, hoaxes, or influenced by cultural beliefs and preconceptions. Nevertheless, these firsthand accounts contribute to the overall narrative surrounding Bigfoot, adding to the collective body of anecdotal evidence and inspiring further investigation and research.

Encountering Bigfoot or believing to have encountered the creature can have significant psychological and emotional impacts on individuals. The experience of encountering an unknown and potentially mythical creature can evoke a range of reactions and responses, shaping one's beliefs, emotions, and even their worldview. Here are some psychological and emotional factors that may come into play:

1. Intrigue and Curiosity:

An encounter or belief in encountering Bigfoot can trigger a sense of intrigue and curiosity. The experience may challenge an individual's existing understanding of the natural world, stimulating a desire for further exploration and investigation. The mystery surrounding Bigfoot can ignite a sense of wonder and captivate the imagination, leading individuals to delve deeper into the lore and research surrounding the creature.

2. Belief and Confirmation Bias:

For individuals who genuinely believe they have encountered Bigfoot, their beliefs can become deeply ingrained and resistant to alternative explanations. Confirmation bias, a cognitive bias where individuals interpret and seek out information that confirms their preexisting beliefs, may come into play. This bias can influence how individuals interpret subsequent experiences, reinforcing their conviction in the reality of their encounter.

3. Cognitive Dissonance and Coping Mechanisms:

Encountering or believing in Bigfoot may create cognitive dissonance for individuals who face skepticism or ridicule from others who do not share their belief. This dissonance arises when there is a conflict between one's beliefs and external evidence or societal norms. In response, individuals may employ coping mechanisms, such as seeking validation from like-minded communities, engaging in research or investigation to reinforce their beliefs, or distancing themselves from skeptical perspectives.

4. Emotional Impact:

The emotional impact of a Bigfoot encounter can vary widely depending on the nature of the experience, individual beliefs, and personal characteristics. Some individuals may experience a mix of awe, excitement, and fear during the encounter itself. Afterward, emotions can range from a sense of validation and empowerment to confusion, anxiety, or even a feeling of being overwhelmed by the encounter. The emotional impact may also depend on cultural and societal factors, as beliefs and attitudes toward mythical creatures differ across cultures.

5. Social Impact and Stigma:

Believing in Bigfoot encounters can lead to social consequences, as individuals may face skepticism, ridicule, or even social ostracism from those who do not share their beliefs. The fear of being stigmatized or dismissed by others may impact an individual's willingness to share their encounter or beliefs openly. This can lead to a sense of isolation and frustration, as individuals seek validation and understanding within communities of like-minded individuals.

6. Personal Growth and Meaning-Making:

For some individuals, encounters with Bigfoot or belief in encountering the creature can be transformative, leading to personal growth and a revised sense of meaning or purpose. These experiences may prompt individuals to question their relationship with the natural world, explore their beliefs about the unknown, and develop a deeper appreciation for the mysteries of the universe. Such encounters can shape personal narratives and become part of an individual's identity or life's purpose.

Encountering Bigfoot or believing in such encounters can have profound psychological and emotional impacts. The experience can evoke curiosity, shape beliefs, trigger cognitive dissonance, and impact individuals' emotional well-being. These encounters may lead to personal growth, foster a sense of belonging within like-minded communities, or generate social challenges due to skepticism or stigma. Understanding the psychological and emotional impact of these encounters contributes to a broader understanding of the significance of Bigfoot in individual lives and the cultural fascination with the creature.

Chapter 16: The Future of Bigfoot Research

In recent years, Bigfoot research has evolved, incorporating emerging theories and areas of study that seek to provide new insights and approaches to understanding the elusive creature. While the existence of Bigfoot remains unproven, these theories and areas of study reflect the ongoing exploration and scientific inquiry surrounding the phenomenon. Here are some emerging theories and areas of study within Bigfoot research:

1. Behavioral Ecology and Habitat Analysis:

Researchers are increasingly focusing on the behavioral ecology of Bigfoot, investigating its potential habitat preferences, movement patterns, and interactions with the environment. By examining ecological factors, such as resource availability, seasonal variations, and habitat suitability, scientists aim to develop a more comprehensive understanding of the creature's behavior and potential distribution.

2. Bioacoustics and Vocalizations:

The study of Bigfoot vocalizations, known as bioacoustics, has gained attention in recent years. Researchers analyze audio recordings to identify distinct vocal patterns, measure acoustic parameters, and compare them to known animal sounds. This field of study aims to determine the nature, purpose, and potential communication systems within the Bigfoot population.

3. Genetics and DNA Analysis:

Advancements in genetic research and DNA analysis techniques have allowed researchers to explore the genetic aspects of Bigfoot. By examining DNA samples attributed to Bigfoot, scientists seek to identify unique genetic markers, conduct population studies, and potentially establish kinship patterns. However, obtaining reliable DNA samples remains a challenge in Bigfoot research.

4. Anthropology and Hominin Evolution:

Some researchers explore the potential connection between Bigfoot and human evolutionary history. Drawing on anthropological and paleontological perspectives, they consider the possibility that Bigfoot could be an undiscovered hominin species, such as a surviving population of Gigantopithecus or an offshoot of the Homo lineage. This approach seeks to link Bigfoot sightings and evidence to the broader context of human evolution.

5. Remote Sensing Technologies:

Advances in remote sensing technologies, such as LiDAR (Light Detection and Ranging) and satellite imagery, have the potential to aid Bigfoot research. LiDAR can create detailed topographic maps, revealing hidden terrain features that could provide clues to Bigfoot habitat preferences. Satellite imagery can assist in monitoring large areas for potential signs of

Bigfoot activity, such as disturbance patterns or anomalous heat signatures.

6. Skepticism and Critical Analysis:

Skepticism and critical analysis continue to be essential components of Bigfoot research. Skeptical researchers approach the subject with a critical eye, questioning evidence, investigating potential hoaxes or misidentifications, and exploring alternative explanations for reported sightings. This approach fosters a rigorous scientific inquiry and helps filter out unreliable or dubious claims.

7. Collaboration and Data Sharing:

With the advent of technology and online platforms, there has been an increased emphasis on collaboration and data sharing within the Bigfoot research community. Researchers and enthusiasts are pooling their resources, sharing sighting data, and collaborating on investigations. This collaborative approach allows for a more comprehensive analysis of evidence and the development of standardized protocols for data collection and analysis.

Emerging theories and areas of study within Bigfoot research reflect the evolving nature of the field. Behavioral ecology, bioacoustics, genetics, anthropology, remote sensing, skepticism, and collaboration are all contributing to a more comprehensive and scientific exploration of the Bigfoot phenomenon. While the existence of Bigfoot remains unproven, these emerging theories and areas of study highlight the ongoing dedication to understanding this elusive creature and the quest for credible evidence in the realm of cryptozoology.

As Bigfoot research continues to evolve, there is ongoing anticipation for potential breakthroughs and the future direction of investigations. While the existence of Bigfoot remains unproven, advancements in technology, interdisciplinary collaboration, and a growing scientific interest in cryptids offer promising avenues for future research. Here are some areas that could lead to potential breakthroughs and shape the future direction of Bigfoot investigations:

1. Advanced DNA Analysis:

Advancements in DNA analysis techniques, such as next-generation sequencing and environmental DNA (eDNA) sampling, could yield significant breakthroughs in Bigfoot research. Improved methods for collecting and analyzing DNA samples, coupled with more extensive genetic databases, may help identify unique genetic markers associated with Bigfoot. Large-scale genetic studies, including population genetics and kinship analyses, could provide valuable insights into the creature's evolutionary history and existence.

2. Artificial Intelligence and Machine Learning:

The application of artificial intelligence (AI) and machine learning algorithms to Bigfoot research holds great potential. These technologies can aid in data analysis, image recognition, and pattern detection. AI algorithms could be trained to analyze vast amounts of audio, visual, and environmental data to identify patterns, classify potential evidence, and refine search strategies. This could help researchers sift through the wealth of anecdotal reports and focus on credible encounters and evidence.

3. Remote Sensing and Geospatial Analysis:

Advancements in remote sensing technologies, such as LiDAR and satellite imagery, combined with geospatial analysis, could enhance the search for Bigfoot. High-resolution aerial and satellite imagery can provide detailed views of remote and inaccessible areas, enabling researchers to identify potential habitat features, track movement patterns, and detect anomalies. LiDAR data, combined with terrain analysis and modeling, can help identify hidden structures or paths that may be associated with Bigfoot activity.

4. Interdisciplinary Collaboration:

Collaboration between different scientific disciplines, such as primatology, wildlife biology, anthropology, and forensics, can foster a more holistic and rigorous approach to Bigfoot research. By pooling expertise, sharing methodologies, and collaborating on investigations, researchers can bring diverse perspectives and methodologies to the table. This interdisciplinary approach can help develop standardized protocols, establish criteria for evidence evaluation, and contribute to a more rigorous scientific study of Bigfoot.

5. Long-Term Monitoring and Field Studies:

Long-term monitoring and field studies focused on known hotspots or areas with high Bigfoot sighting reports could provide valuable insights into the creature's behavior, habitat use, and potential population dynamics. Employing camera traps, acoustic monitoring devices, and other remote sensing technologies for extended periods can increase the chances of capturing credible evidence and help researchers better understand Bigfoot's elusive nature.

6. Public Participation and Citizen Science:

The involvement of the public through citizen science initiatives can broaden the scope of Bigfoot research. Engaging a network of citizen scientists to report sightings, collect evidence, and contribute to data collection efforts can provide a more extensive and diverse dataset for analysis. Crowdsourcing and community engagement can also foster public awareness, interest, and support for Bigfoot research.

7. Ethical Considerations and Conservation:

As Bigfoot investigations progress, ethical considerations regarding the potential impact on the creature's well-being and conservation become increasingly important. Researchers must address ethical guidelines and protocols to ensure the welfare of both the research subjects and the ecosystems they inhabit. Promoting responsible and sustainable research practices, respectful engagement with indigenous communities, and the preservation of natural habitats can contribute to a more ethical and scientifically rigorous approach to Bigfoot investigations.

The future direction of Bigfoot investigations holds exciting possibilities. Advancements in DNA analysis, AI, remote sensing, interdisciplinary collaboration, long-term monitoring, and citizen science can contribute to potential breakthroughs and a more systematic study of Bigfoot. As technology and scientific methodologies continue to advance, researchers have an opportunity to explore new frontiers, refine investigative techniques, and address unanswered questions surrounding the existence and nature of this enduring mystery.

Chapter 17: Unraveling the Mystery of Bigfoot

Throughout the book "Bigfoot: The Comprehensive Investigation into the Elusive Legend," we have delved into various aspects of Bigfoot research, presenting findings, arguments, and perspectives surrounding the phenomenon. Here is a summary of the key points discussed:

1. Historical and Cultural References: We explored the historical and cultural references to Bigfoot, including ancient legends, folklore, and indigenous mythology. These references highlight the long-standing presence of Bigfoot-like creatures in human cultures and their significance in local lore.

2. Characteristics and Physical Features: We examined the commonly associated characteristics and physical features of Bigfoot, including its large size, bipedal locomotion, covered in hair, and reported ape-like or human-like features. These descriptions form the basis of eyewitness accounts and contribute to the composite image of Bigfoot.

3. Eyewitness Accounts: We analyzed various eyewitness accounts, highlighting their similarities in describing the creature's appearance, behavior, and vocalizations. While individual accounts vary, the consistency in these reports adds to the body of anecdotal evidence surrounding Bigfoot.

4. Field of Cryptozoology: We introduced the field of cryptozoology and its relation to Bigfoot. Cryptozoology explores the existence of undiscovered or hidden animals, and Bigfoot is one of the prime subjects of interest within this field.

5. Other Cryptids: We discussed other famous cryptids, such as the Loch Ness Monster and the Yeti, and drew parallels to Bigfoot. These cryptids share similarities in terms of the elusive nature and cultural significance attached to them.

6. Famous Bigfoot Sightings: We provided an overview of notable Bigfoot sightings throughout history, including the Ape Canyon Incident, the Albert Ostman abduction, and the Patterson-Gimlin film. These sightings have contributed to the popularization and ongoing interest in Bigfoot.

7. Credible Evidence: We examined various forms of evidence, such as footprints, photographs, and video footage, and discussed their validity and limitations in the context of Bigfoot research. While some evidence is compelling, it is crucial to critically analyze and scrutinize it to separate genuine encounters from misidentifications or hoaxes.

8. Expeditions and Research Efforts: We explored notable expeditions and research efforts dedicated to finding Bigfoot, including field investigations, long-term monitoring projects, and collaborations among researchers. These efforts aim to gather systematic data, document encounters, and contribute to the body of knowledge surrounding Bigfoot.

9. Technological Advancements: We discussed the role of modern technology, such as drones, thermal imaging, and

DNA analysis, in aiding Bigfoot research. These advancements enhance data collection, analysis, and documentation, providing researchers with new tools to investigate potential encounters and evidence.

10. Scientific Community and Skepticism: We examined the scientific community's perception of Bigfoot and the skeptical viewpoints and arguments against its existence. While some researchers remain open-minded, others approach the subject with skepticism, emphasizing the importance of critical thinking and scientific rigor in evaluating claims.

11. Indigenous Cultures: We explored the significance of Bigfoot in indigenous cultures, highlighting their rich mythology, beliefs, and cultural practices associated with similar creatures. Indigenous perspectives provide valuable insights into the longstanding connection between humans and cryptid folklore.

12. Pop Culture and Tourism: We traced the portrayal of Bigfoot in movies, literature, and media, emphasizing its enduring appeal and influence on popular culture. We also explored regions renowned for Bigfoot sightings and associated tourism, where festivals, attractions, and local folklore contribute to the fascination with the creature.

13. Future Directions: Lastly, we discussed emerging theories and areas of study within Bigfoot research, including behavioral ecology, genetics, remote sensing, interdisciplinary collaboration, and ethical considerations. These areas offer potential breakthroughs and shape the future direction of investigations.

Throughout the book, we presented a wide range of perspectives, evidence, and theories surrounding Bigfoot. While the existence of Bigfoot remains unproven, the ongoing research and exploration contribute to the scientific and cultural understanding of this elusive legend.

The enduring allure of Bigfoot lies in its status as a captivating enigma that challenges our understanding of the natural world. Despite the lack of definitive scientific evidence, the fascination with Bigfoot persists, captivating the imaginations of individuals across cultures and generations. This enduring allure stems from several factors and has a profound impact on our understanding of the natural world.

Firstly, Bigfoot represents the unknown, tapping into the innate human curiosity about hidden creatures and mysteries lurking in unexplored wilderness areas. It sparks a sense of wonder and possibility, fueling a desire to explore and discover the secrets of our world. Bigfoot's elusive nature and limited scientific documentation create an air of uncertainty and leave room for the imagination to fill the gaps, contributing to its enduring allure.

Secondly, Bigfoot challenges conventional scientific knowledge and pushes the boundaries of what we consider possible. Its existence, if proven, would require a reevaluation of our understanding of primate evolution, biodiversity, and the limits of undiscovered species. The prospect of uncovering a creature that has managed to evade detection in our modern age ignites the imagination and challenges our assumptions about the natural world.

Furthermore, Bigfoot serves as a cultural touchstone, connecting us to our collective past and ancestral legends. References to similar creatures can be found in indigenous cultures and folklore worldwide, reinforcing the notion that Bigfoot is not merely a modern construct but a longstanding part of human mythology. Its enduring presence in popular culture through movies, books, and media further solidifies its place in our collective consciousness.

The impact of Bigfoot on our understanding of the natural world is multifaceted. It prompts questions about the limits of scientific knowledge, the existence of undiscovered species, and the interplay between folklore and reality. The ongoing investigation into Bigfoot has sparked interdisciplinary collaboration, with researchers from various fields exploring its potential existence. This interdisciplinary approach expands our understanding of the natural world, encouraging the integration of different perspectives, methodologies, and technologies in the pursuit of answers.

Bigfoot's enduring allure also underscores the importance of keeping an open mind and embracing curiosity in scientific exploration. While skepticism and critical thinking are crucial, the allure of mysteries like Bigfoot reminds us of the value of exploring uncharted territory, both physically and intellectually. It serves as a reminder that there is still much to learn and discover, even in familiar landscapes.

The enduring allure of Bigfoot lies in its ability to ignite our curiosity, challenge scientific boundaries, and connect us to the mysteries of our past. It serves as a cultural symbol and a catalyst for interdisciplinary research, inspiring us to explore the unknown and expand our understanding of the natural world. While the search for Bigfoot continues, its impact extends beyond the realm of cryptozoology, influencing our perception of what is possible and deepening our appreciation for the wonders that still await discovery.

Chapter 18: Bigfoot and Beyond: Other Cryptids

The world is rich with tales of mysterious creatures and cryptids, creatures whose existence is unsubstantiated by mainstream science but are subjects of fascination and folklore. Here is an overview of some notable examples from various regions around the world:

1. Loch Ness Monster (Nessie):

One of the most famous cryptids, the Loch Ness Monster, is said to inhabit Loch Ness, a deep freshwater loch in Scotland. Descriptions depict Nessie as a large aquatic creature resembling a plesiosaur, with a long neck and humps emerging from the water. Sightings and alleged photographs have fueled speculation and extensive investigations, making Nessie an enduring mystery.

2. Yeti (Abominable Snowman):

The Yeti is a legendary creature believed to roam the snowy Himalayan mountains of Nepal, Tibet, and Bhutan. Described as an ape-like creature, the Yeti is said to possess incredible strength and live in remote, rugged terrain. Numerous reports of footprints, sightings, and local folklore have contributed to its enduring presence in the cultural imagination.

3. Chupacabra:

The Chupacabra, meaning "goat-sucker" in Spanish, is a creature primarily reported in the Americas, particularly Puerto Rico, Mexico, and the United States. It is described as a reptilian or canine-like creature that attacks and drains the blood of livestock, especially goats. Sightings have led to speculations ranging from unknown creatures to misidentified animals or urban legends.

4. Mothman:

The Mothman is associated with a series of sightings that occurred in Point Pleasant, West Virginia, in the late 1960s. Described as a winged humanoid creature with glowing red eyes, the Mothman was said to be associated with premonitions of disaster, including the collapse of the Silver Bridge. The legend of the Mothman continues to intrigue and inspire curiosity.

5. Jersey Devil:

The Jersey Devil is a creature of folklore said to inhabit the Pine Barrens of southern New Jersey, United States. It is described as a winged creature with a goat-like or horse-like head, hooves, and bat-like wings. Legends surrounding the Jersey Devil date back centuries, and sightings continue to be reported, though explanations range from misidentifications to urban legends.

6. Yowie:

The Yowie is an Australian cryptid believed to inhabit the remote forests and wilderness areas of Australia. Descriptions vary, but it is generally depicted as a large, hairy, bipedal creature similar to Bigfoot or the Yeti. Indigenous Australian folklore includes tales of Yowie-like creatures, adding cultural significance to the mystery.

7. Orang Pendek:

The Orang Pendek is a cryptid reported in the dense forests of Sumatra, Indonesia. Described as a short-statured, bipedal ape-like creature, the Orang Pendek has gained attention from cryptozoologists and researchers. Limited evidence, including footprints and eyewitness accounts, fuels ongoing investigations into its potential existence.

8. Mokele-Mbembe:

The Mokele-Mbembe is a creature of Central African folklore, said to inhabit the swamps and rivers of the Congo Basin. Descriptions range from a sauropod-like creature to a large reptilian or elephant-like creature. Expeditions and investigations into the Mokele-Mbembe continue, with efforts to gather evidence and document the creature's existence.

These are just a few examples of the many mysterious creatures and cryptids found across the globe. Each one carries its own unique mythology, cultural significance, and ongoing investigation. While scientific evidence for their existence remains elusive, they continue to captivate the human imagination, sparking curiosity and fueling the pursuit of understanding the mysteries that lie beyond our current knowledge.

Many of the mysterious creatures and cryptids mentioned share similarities with Bigfoot, both in terms of their characteristics and the potential for further investigation. These similarities include:

1. Elusive Nature: Like Bigfoot, these creatures are often described as elusive and difficult to capture or study. They are reported to inhabit remote or inaccessible areas, making it challenging to gather concrete evidence of their existence.

2. Folklore and Cultural Significance: Similar to Bigfoot, these creatures have deep roots in folklore and cultural beliefs. They are often part of local legends and oral traditions, passed down through generations. Investigating their existence can provide insights into cultural narratives and the ways in which folklore shapes our understanding of the natural world.

3. Eyewitness Accounts: Sightings and encounters form a significant part of the evidence surrounding these cryptids. Eyewitness accounts describe similar physical characteristics, behaviors, and habitat preferences, providing a basis for comparison and analysis.

4. Potential for Scientific Investigation: Just like Bigfoot, these cryptids offer opportunities for scientific investigation. Researchers can employ various methodologies, including field surveys, DNA analysis, audio recordings, and footprint analysis, to gather evidence and potentially shed light on their existence.

5. Interdisciplinary Collaboration: Investigating these cryptids often requires interdisciplinary collaboration.

Researchers from fields such as zoology, anthropology, genetics, and ecology can join forces to conduct comprehensive studies, combining their expertise and methodologies to approach the mystery from multiple angles.

6. Technological Advancements: Advances in technology, such as DNA analysis, remote sensing, and data collection tools, can aid in the investigation of these cryptids. These tools can help gather more accurate and precise data, analyze audio and visual recordings, and map their potential habitats.

7. Conservation and Biodiversity: Investigating these cryptids has broader implications for conservation and biodiversity. It highlights the need to explore and protect remote and untouched wilderness areas that may harbor undiscovered species. These investigations can contribute to our understanding of ecosystem dynamics and the importance of preserving biodiversity hotspots.

While the scientific consensus remains skeptical about the existence of these cryptids, the similarities to Bigfoot and the potential for further investigation provide avenues for scientific exploration, cultural understanding, and ecological conservation. By approaching these cryptids with a rigorous scientific mindset, employing advanced methodologies, and fostering interdisciplinary collaboration, researchers can expand our knowledge of the natural world and unravel the mysteries that continue to capture our imaginations.

Chapter 19: Bigfoot: Fact or Fiction?

The existence of Bigfoot, like many cryptids, remains a subject of debate and speculation. The evidence both for and against its existence has been scrutinized and analyzed by researchers and enthusiasts alike. Here is a balanced analysis of the evidence for and against the existence of Bigfoot:

Evidence For the Existence of Bigfoot:

1. Eyewitness Accounts: There are numerous eyewitness accounts from individuals who claim to have encountered Bigfoot. These accounts often share similarities in describing the creature's appearance, behavior, and vocalizations. While individual accounts can be subjective, the collective consistency across different locations and time periods provides anecdotal support for the existence of Bigfoot.

2. Footprints: Many alleged Bigfoot footprints have been discovered, exhibiting characteristics such as large size, distinct dermal ridges, and a midtarsal break. Some casts have been subjected to expert analysis, which suggests that they cannot be easily dismissed as hoaxes or misidentifications. However, skeptics argue that footprint evidence can be fabricated or misinterpreted.

3. Audio Recordings: There have been numerous audio recordings capturing purported Bigfoot vocalizations. These

recordings feature distinct, often haunting sounds that do not correspond to known wildlife or human vocalizations. While the authenticity and interpretation of these recordings are debated, they contribute to the body of evidence supporting the existence of an unidentified creature.

4. Visual Evidence: Photographs and video footage claiming to depict Bigfoot have been captured over the years. The most famous example is the Patterson-Gimlin film, which shows a figure resembling a large bipedal creature walking through a forest. While skeptics question the authenticity of some visual evidence, these images contribute to the ongoing fascination and belief in Bigfoot.

Evidence Against the Existence of Bigfoot:

1. Lack of Physical Evidence: Despite decades of investigation, no conclusive physical evidence has been obtained to definitively prove the existence of Bigfoot. Skeptics argue that the absence of bones, DNA samples, or clear and unambiguous photographs raises doubts about the creature's existence. The lack of verifiable physical evidence remains a significant hurdle in establishing its reality.

2. Hoaxes and Misidentifications: The prevalence of hoaxes and misidentifications raises skepticism about Bigfoot sightings and evidence. Some individuals have confessed to fabricating evidence or perpetrating hoaxes for personal gain or attention. Additionally, misidentifications of known animals, such as bears or large primates, can contribute to false reports and distort the perception of Bigfoot sightings.

3. Limited Scientific Support: The scientific community generally remains skeptical of Bigfoot's existence due to the lack of scientifically accepted evidence. The absence of peer-reviewed studies, the scarcity of credible experts dedicating their research to the subject, and the perceived lack of rigorous methodology in investigations contribute to the scientific skepticism.

4. Implausibility and Lack of Reproducibility: The concept of a large, undiscovered hominid species existing in various regions without being captured or leaving irrefutable evidence challenges the principles of biology, ecology, and population dynamics. The inability to reproduce sightings or encounters under controlled conditions further weakens the case for Bigfoot's existence.

The evidence for and against the existence of Bigfoot presents a complex and contested landscape. While eyewitness accounts, footprints, audio recordings, and visual evidence contribute to the belief in Bigfoot, skeptics highlight the lack of conclusive physical evidence, the prevalence of hoaxes, and the scientific skepticism surrounding the subject. The enduring allure of Bigfoot, however, continues to fuel research, inspire investigations, and spark curiosity about the mysteries that may still be uncovered in our natural world.

In light of the evidence and arguments presented regarding the existence of Bigfoot, it is essential to encourage readers to draw their own conclusions based on the available information. The topic of Bigfoot is characterized by a wide range of viewpoints, speculation, and ongoing debate within both scientific and public communities. While the evidence for and against Bigfoot's existence has been discussed, no definitive proof has emerged thus far.

As readers, it is crucial to approach this subject with an open and critical mind, evaluating the evidence, considering different perspectives, and examining the methodologies employed in research and investigations. Engaging in constructive dialogue and considering the strengths and weaknesses of various arguments can lead to a more comprehensive understanding of the topic.

It is important to remember that belief in the existence of Bigfoot often extends beyond empirical evidence, encompassing personal experiences, cultural beliefs, and the allure of the unknown. While science strives to provide concrete answers based on verifiable evidence, some phenomena remain elusive and may require further exploration or breakthroughs in research methodologies.

Ultimately, the decision to believe in or reject the existence of Bigfoot rests with each individual. It is an opportunity to embrace curiosity, engage in thoughtful inquiry, and form personal opinions based on the available information. Whether you find the evidence compelling, remain skeptical, or hold an agnostic stance, the journey of exploration and critical thinking is as valuable as the destination.

Regardless of individual conclusions, the enduring fascination with Bigfoot continues to inspire investigations, fuel scientific inquiry, and contribute to the rich tapestry of human culture and folklore. By approaching the subject with an open mind and a willingness to engage in respectful discourse, readers can actively participate in the ongoing exploration of this captivating mystery.

Chapter 20: The Legacy of Bigfoot

The Bigfoot phenomenon has left a significant cultural and scientific legacy that spans decades. Its impact can be observed in various realms, influencing popular culture, scientific inquiry, and our understanding of the natural world. Here, we reflect on the enduring legacy of the Bigfoot phenomenon:

Cultural Legacy:

1. Folklore and Mythology: Bigfoot has become an integral part of folklore and mythology, not only in North America but also in other parts of the world. The creature's legend has been passed down through generations, contributing to local lore, indigenous traditions, and oral histories. Bigfoot's enduring presence in cultural narratives reflects humanity's fascination with the unknown and our desire to explain the mysteries of the natural world.

2. Popular Culture: Bigfoot's impact on popular culture is undeniable. It has become a prominent figure in books, movies, documentaries, television shows, and even video games. Countless portrayals of Bigfoot have captivated audiences, further fueling the creature's cultural significance. The creature's image has been used in advertisements, merchandise, and as a symbol of mystery and adventure.

3. Tourism and Local Economy: Regions renowned for Bigfoot sightings have embraced the creature's cultural allure, leveraging it for tourism and local economies. Festivals, attractions, and museums dedicated to Bigfoot attract enthusiasts, tourists, and curious visitors. These events and destinations not only provide entertainment but also contribute to the local economy, fostering a sense of community and identity.

Scientific Legacy:

1. Cryptozoology and Investigative Science: Bigfoot's existence has given rise to the field of cryptozoology, which explores hidden or unknown animals. Although cryptozoology remains a subject of debate within the scientific community, the study of Bigfoot has spurred research, investigations, and interdisciplinary collaboration. The legacy of Bigfoot in scientific inquiry demonstrates the human desire to explore the unexplained and push the boundaries of knowledge.

2. Conservation and Biodiversity: Bigfoot's existence, or the quest to prove or disprove it, has brought attention to the importance of preserving natural habitats and biodiversity. The search for Bigfoot often takes researchers to remote and pristine wilderness areas, promoting the need to protect these ecosystems. The legacy of Bigfoot in conservation underscores the interconnectedness between mysterious creatures, their habitats, and the broader natural world.

3. Skepticism and Critical Thinking: The Bigfoot phenomenon has fostered a spirit of skepticism and critical

thinking. It serves as a reminder to approach extraordinary claims with a scientific mindset, encouraging the evaluation of evidence, the application of rigorous methodologies, and the careful consideration of alternative explanations. The legacy of Bigfoot in skepticism promotes a healthy skepticism and skepticism and the need for empirical evidence in scientific inquiry.

The cultural and scientific legacy of the Bigfoot phenomenon is multi-faceted and far-reaching. Bigfoot has left an indelible mark on folklore, popular culture, and local economies, becoming an iconic figure in our collective imagination. Scientifically, Bigfoot has sparked investigations, interdisciplinary collaboration, and discussions on conservation and critical thinking. Whether one believes in Bigfoot's existence or remains skeptical, the phenomenon's legacy continues to inspire curiosity, challenge our understanding of the natural world, and serve as a testament to humanity's enduring fascination with the unknown.

The Bigfoot phenomenon has had a profound impact on our understanding of the unknown and the possibilities that lie ahead. It serves as a reminder that there are still mysteries to be unraveled in the natural world and challenges us to explore beyond the boundaries of what is currently known. Here, we reflect on the impact of Bigfoot on our understanding of the unknown and the potential it holds for future discoveries:

1. Curiosity and Exploration: The existence of Bigfoot fuels our innate curiosity and desire to explore the unknown. It reminds us that there are still uncharted territories, both in

remote wilderness areas and within the depths of our own consciousness. The pursuit of understanding Bigfoot encourages us to venture into unexplored regions, embracing the spirit of exploration and expanding our understanding of the natural world.

2. Biodiversity and Unexplored Species: The possibility of Bigfoot's existence opens up a realm of potential discoveries in terms of biodiversity and undiscovered species. It highlights the idea that there may be large, elusive creatures yet to be documented by science. The pursuit of Bigfoot encourages us to consider the vastness and complexity of the natural world and the potential for future revelations about its diverse inhabitants.

3. Interdisciplinary Collaboration: Bigfoot research often involves collaboration between different scientific disciplines, including biology, anthropology, ecology, and more. This interdisciplinary approach fosters new perspectives, methodologies, and insights into understanding the unknown. It encourages scientists to work together, combining their expertise to tackle complex mysteries and contribute to a more holistic understanding of our world.

4. Technological Advancements: The quest for Bigfoot has prompted the development and application of advanced technologies in research and exploration. From thermal imaging cameras and drones to DNA analysis and remote sensing techniques, technological advancements aid in data collection, analysis, and documentation. The pursuit of Bigfoot

drives the push for innovative tools and methodologies that can be applied to other areas of scientific inquiry.

5. Open-Mindedness and Paradigm Shifts: The existence of Bigfoot challenges our preconceived notions and encourages open-mindedness in scientific inquiry. It serves as a reminder that the unknown can challenge established paradigms and lead to paradigm shifts in our understanding of the natural world. The pursuit of Bigfoot compels us to approach mysteries with a willingness to question existing frameworks and embrace new possibilities.

6. Preservation of Wilderness and Cultural Heritage: Bigfoot's existence, or the quest to uncover it, highlights the importance of preserving wilderness areas and cultural heritage. The pursuit of Bigfoot often takes researchers into remote and pristine ecosystems, emphasizing the need for conservation and the protection of natural habitats. It also encourages the preservation of indigenous cultural narratives and practices that hold valuable knowledge about the natural world.

The Bigfoot phenomenon has a significant impact on our understanding of the unknown and the possibilities that lie ahead. It inspires curiosity, fosters interdisciplinary collaboration, encourages technological advancements, and challenges existing paradigms. The pursuit of Bigfoot reminds us that there is still much to be explored and discovered in our world, inviting us to embrace the unknown with open minds and to continue pushing the boundaries of scientific exploration.

Sign up to my free newsletter to get updates on new releases, FREE teaser chapters to upcoming releases and FREE digital short stories.

Or visit https://tinyurl.com/olanc

I never spam and you can unsubscribe at any time.

Don't miss out!

Visit the website below and you can sign up to receive emails whenever Oliver Lancaster publishes a new book. There's no charge and no obligation.

https://books2read.com/r/B-A-UNEZ-WPLLC

BOOKS 2 READ

Connecting independent readers to independent writers.

Also by Oliver Lancaster

Chernobyl: Unveiling the tragedy. A Comprehensive Account of the Nuclear Disaster

The Bhopal Gas Tragedy: Unraveling the Catastrophe of 1984

The Deepwater Horizon Oil Spill of 2010: A Disaster Unveiled

Fukushima Fallout: Unveiling the Truth behind the 2011 Nuclear Disaster

Minamata Disease: Poisoned Waters and the Battle for Justice (1932-1968)

Evil Women: Unmasking History's Most Notorious Women

Bundy The Dark Chronicles: America's Infamous Serial Killer

Dahmer The Dark Chronicles: America's Infamous Milwaukee Cannibal

Zodiac The Dark Chronicles: America's Infamous Cryptic Killer

Bigfoot: The Comprehensive Investigation into the Elusive Legend

Watch for more at https://tinyurl.com/olanc.

About the Author

Oliver Lancaster possesses an enchanting charm that effortlessly draws readers into the depths of his literary world. With an insatiable curiosity for the unexplained, he skillfully weaves tales of crime, conspiracy, mystery and the unknown, leaving readers on the edge of their seats.

Nestled away in the seclusion of his garden shed, Oliver finds solace and inspiration in the tranquility of nature. Surrounded by greenery and fragrant blooms, he dives into a realm of imagination, unearthing secrets that lie hidden within his mind.

Accompanying Oliver on his literary ventures is his faithful ginger cat named Italics. With his mesmerizing gaze and mysterious mannerisms, Italics adds an air of intrigue to Oliver's writing process, often curling up on a cushioned chair nearby, watching as words flow effortlessly from his human companion's pen.

When not engrossed in his craft, Oliver indulges in the gentle warmth of his garden with a glass of red wine.

Prepare to be spellbound as you delve into the pages of Oliver Lancaster's novels, for he is a master of the eerie, a weaver of secrets, and an unrivaled guide through the labyrinthine corridors of the human psyche.

Sign up to a free newsletter to get updates on new releases, FREE teaser chapters to upcoming releases and FREE digital short stories.

Read more at https://tinyurl.com/olanc.